P9-DCQ-190

TEACHER'S Discovery®

Research Paper Procedure
HIGH SCHOOL

by Amy M. Kleppner
and Cynthia Skelton

Includes changes from

**MLA Handbook for Writers of Research Papers
Seventh Edition (2009) by the Modern Language Association of America**

and

**Publication Manual of the American Psychological Association (APA)
Sixth Edition (2009)**

Published by:
Teacher's Discovery®

2676 Paldan Drive
Auburn Hills, MI 48326
www.teachersdiscovery.com

To order English/language arts materials:
Teacher's Discovery® English Division   Phone: 1-800-583-6454
2676 Paldan Drive, Suite A   Fax: 1-888-395-6686
Auburn Hills, MI 48326

To order social studies materials:
Teacher's Discovery® Social Studies Division   Phone: 1-800-543-4180
2676 Paldan Drive, Suite B   Fax: 1-888-395-1492
Auburn Hills, MI 48326

To order science materials:
Teacher's Discovery® Science Division   Phone: 1-888-977-2436
2676 Paldan Drive, Suite C   Fax: 1-888-987-2436
Auburn Hills, MI 48326

To order foreign language materials:
Teacher's Discovery®
Foreign Language Division   Phone: 1-800-832-2437
2741 Paldan Drive   Fax: 1-800-287-4509
Auburn Hills, MI 48326

Publication Manager: Nancy W. Cracknell
Cover Design: Nancy W. Cracknell
Desktop Publisher: Michelle Bock

Copyright © 1997, 2001, 2002, 2004, 2007, 2009. Teacher's Discovery®,
a division of the American Eagle Company, Inc.

All rights reserved, including the right of
reproduction in whole or in part in any form.

SKU: TB1308E
ISBN: 978-0-7560-1197-0

Acknowledgements

It is a pleasure to acknowledge the valued contributors who aided in the creation of this manual.

Adam Kleppner, Bram Kleppner, Caleb Kleppner, Caroline James, Dr. Jerome Marco, Ginny Trulio, Jason Rosensweig, Jeffrey Dickinson, Jo Tunstall, Lisa Baker, Margaret Marple, Marjorie Geldon, Penny Mayorga, Portia Cornell, Witt J. Farquhar, and Walt Whitman High School in Bethesda, Maryland.

Amy M. Kleppner

Further acknowledgements for the third edition go to Ronnie Foreman, Kevin Xu, and Sarah Cha, students whose noteworthy scholarship provides the model papers in Appendix C. Thank you as well to Jane Kessner and the teachers from Walt Whitman High School and other schools, whose insights, experiences, and expertise contributed to the revision of this book.

Cynthia Skelton

© 2009. Teacher's Discovery®

Letter to the Student

During your four years in high school, you will have the opportunity to do research in many fields. You may want to give an informative speech in an English class, perhaps on the evolution of football, or maybe on the psychology of roller coaster construction. Your biology teacher may assign a debate on an issue in bioethics, for example, to present the arguments for or against doctor-assisted suicide. You may decide to write a paper showing how Jack London used his own adventurous life in writing his fiction; to present a dramatic monologue by an American sailor captured by the British during the War of 1812; or to provide the commentary for a slide show on action-in-repose in Michelangelo's slave sculptures. Or perhaps you're considering a PowerPoint presentation on the dangers of using the drug Ecstasy.

The purpose of this manual is to provide guidelines to help you complete these projects successfully. Your research will take you first to your school's media center, and that will link you to an amazing variety of sources beyond the books, magazines, newspapers, pamphlets, reprints of articles, and other material available there. Research today is a global endeavor, and you are likely to uncover much more information than you can possibly use. And that is only the beginning: beyond the electronic links to county and university libraries, to databases covering every conceivable subject, and to CD-ROMs and websites, there are dozens of other information sources, including interviews, surveys, family histories, videos, films, and recordings.

You will discover the many pleasures of doing research: the excitement of discovering new material; the fun of working independently; the satisfaction of producing a well-organized paper from a chaos of note cards, printouts, outlines, and preliminary drafts. And you'll acquire skills that will serve you throughout your life. As a professional, you may conduct research in science, medicine, law, social science, or the humanities. On a personal level, you may want to trace your family's roots through genealogical research. As a community activist, you may need to study your city's budget for education or the area's transportation needs.

Welcome to the world of scholarship, research, and intellectual growth.

Amy M. Kleppner

Table of Contents

© 2009. Teacher's Discovery®

Content

© 2009. Teacher's Discovery®

Content

Introduction

Research Paper Procedure

© 2009. Teacher's Discovery®

Overview of the Research Process

This chapter provides an overview of the whole research process; it maps the journey. It shows the ten steps to be taken from starting point to destination, and it emphasizes the amount of time and effort that executing an excellent paper requires. The chapters that follow provide a detailed description of each step, along with suggestions for avoiding roadblocks and breakdowns.

Any research project is an endeavor requiring careful planning and time management, so understanding the major components will allow the establishment of a series of deadlines to ensure that research is kept on track. These ten steps comprise the backbone of the entire research progress and provide an overview of all the tasks needing completion in order to submit a superior final product. Despite its undeniable appeal, waiting to begin work until the night before a paper is due is likely to result in both a low grade and the knowledge that a better job could have been done.

Steps to Writing a Research Paper

Step 1. Understand the Available Resources.
Become familiar with primary and secondary sources, as well as the variety of print, non-print, and electronic resources that are available. Understand how to locate these resources and how to use them responsibly and without plagiarism.

Step 2. Select a Topic.
Locate a subject of personal interest, then find a specific angle or approach to that topic that is reasonable to handle within the prescribed page limit.

Step 3. Conduct Preliminary Research and Begin Writing Source Cards.
Search for sources of information and record publication information about available resources on source cards, following MLA or APA format.

Step 4. Formulate a Thesis Statement.
After collecting some preliminary information, formulate a judgment, evaluation, or criticism that will serve as the main point, or the thesis, of the paper.

Step 5. Make a Preliminary Outline.
Continue doing research until three to five major topics have been acquired to support the thesis. Then start finding specific supporting evidence for each major supporting topic. Compose a tentative topic outline showing what information is collected and what information still needs to be gathered.

Step 6. Take Notes.
Locate more sources and begin taking notes on note cards, selecting only relevant information and entering it only under the appropriate topic headings on your note cards.

Step 7. Prepare to Write.
Once there is sufficient information, organize note cards under the major supporting topics and return to the outline. Fill in the facts, examples, statistics, and expert opinions that support each major supporting topic. Review the guidelines for incorporating borrowed material into the paper, with particular focus on paraphrasing, summarizing, direct quotation, and parenthetical citations.

© 2009. Teacher's Discovery®

Step 8.   Write the Rough Draft.

With the completed outline and the information on note cards in hand, start writing the rough draft, putting in documentation for all borrowed material. Provide discussion of borrowed material by incorporating insight and analysis. Compose the introductory and concluding paragraphs.

Step 9.   Revise and Proofread.

Self-edit the paper, and then have others edit it. Study the feedback received, then revise. Good writing almost always requires several drafts and several revisions. Use a checklist to guide the revisions.

Step 10. Prepare Works Cited Page.

Prepare your works cited or reference page using the sources that were actually used in the paper. Double check the citation forms and punctuation conventions.

Submit papers on time and with pride. Make sure every paper is an example of honest effort and hard work.

Making a Plan

Understanding each of the steps and the tasks involved in completing each one allows the researcher to set reasonable deadlines so that work moves forward in a steady, deliberate way. Naturally, the amount of time required for any one step will vary according to the specific demands of a particular assignment and an individual's skill set. In addition, the steps are not actually discrete but blend and overlap so that many tasks are actually on-going through continuous steps. For these reasons the researcher should always plan each project anew, instead of relying on a formula to guide deadline decisions. The pie chart below provides a suggestion of how to apportion time by estimating what percentage of the total time spent on the research paper should be dedicated to each step. Students should view this only as a general guideline that may help them determine what kind of due dates to set for themselves as they create their own plan of action.

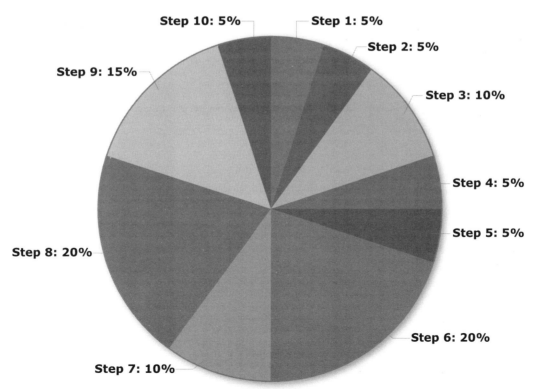

© 2009. Teacher's Discovery®

	Step	Decription
1	Understand the available resources.	Review types of resources, visit the school library, explore public and university library catalogues, and understand how to avoid plagiarism.
2	Select a topic.	Find a topic, read reference materials to get a general overview of your topic, determine an angle, and narrow the topic to suit the assignment.
3	Do preliminary research and begin writing source cards.	Locate valuable sources of information for your narrowed topic, read for ideas about thesis and topic headings, and record data about valuable resources on source cards.
4	Formulate a thesis statement.	Propose a judgment, criticism, or evaluation about your topic, and identify the main topics which will support this tentative thesis.
5	Make a tentative topic outline.	Continue researching and recording information on source cards, find specific supporting evidence for your main topics, and create a tentative outline to guide your note taking.
6	Take notes.	Continue finding sources and recording information on source cards, but begin strategically selecting specific and relevant information to record on note cards.
7	Extend topic outline.	Return to your tentative topic outline, revise thesis, write topic sentences for body sections, and fill in subtopics and supporting evidence with information from your note cards.
8	Write rough draft.	Compose your paper, incorporating and citing your research, as well as your own insight and analysis.
9	Edit and revise.	Re-read your paper and make corrections, ask others to read your paper and provide feedback, use the checklist to ensure that your writing is strong and your citations are correct.
10	Prepare works cited page.	Consult the forms provided or use the MLA/APA handbooks for guidance, and prepare according to correct procedures a works cited or reference page listing the works actually used in your paper.

Submit your paper on time and with pride, knowing that it is your best work.

A Plan of Action worksheet is located in Appendix A on page 144.

© 2009. Teacher's Discovery®

Note:

As the Contents page indicates, this manual provides two forms for the documentation of research papers: the first is the form the Modern Language Association (MLA) recommends[1]; the second is the form the American Psychological Association (APA) recommends.[2]

The MLA is an organization of teachers and scholars, founded in 1883 to strengthen teaching in languages and literature. It developed the *MLA Handbook* to simplify the task of preparing both student papers and scholarly works. The majority of scholarly publications in languages and literature follow MLA guidelines, as do many schools and colleges.

The APA, also an organization of teachers and scholars, promotes research and scholarship in psychology. Its *Publication Manual* is a widely recognized authority for publications in the social sciences. To accommodate the science and social studies departments in many schools, this manual provides APA rules and models as well.

There are other authorities on these matters, and in college *The Chicago Manual of Style* or a manual prepared by the college or university may be the preferred guide.

Regardless of the method they advocate, the goal of all style manuals is the same: to make it easier to convey information with consistency, clarity, accuracy, and honesty.

---

[1] *MLA Handbook for Writers of Research Papers.* 7th ed. New York: Modern Language Association, 2009. See also the MLA Handbook webpage (http://mlahandbook.org), accessible with the code printed on the back flap of the print version of the MLA Handbook.

[2] American Psychological Association, *Publication Manual of the American Psychological Association*, 6th ed. (Washington, DC: APA, 2009). See also the APA *Publication Manual* website. (http://www.apastyle.org/elecref.html)

© 2009. Teacher's Discovery®

Step 1

Resources

Understanding Available Resources

Using Resources Responsibly — Avoiding Plagiarism

© 2009. Teacher's Discovery®

When embarking on a research project, the first impulse of many people is to type some keywords into Google™ and see what results. While Google™ searching is certainly useful in many circumstances, it is not an effective or efficient way to conduct scholarly research. The popular search engines promote content based on the number of hits that a site generates, how that site's html code is written, and the amount of advertising dollars spent. These are not good foundations for producing trustworthy information. Additionally, many search engines cannot access protected sites where the most valuable information may be found. In order to efficiently use one's energy while researching a project, one should avoid the voluminous and disorganized search results of the typical search engine, as well as the unavoidable time spent evaluating the relevance and the quality of its information.

"Did you say Wikipedia?" Wikipedia is not a definitive encyclopedia! It should never be considered as an authoritative source, nor should it be used as a resource for quoting, paraphrasing, or summarizing in a research paper. Their tag line reads "Welcome to Wikipedia, the free encyclopedia *that anyone can edit*." There are over 75,000 active volunteers worldwide contributing to its content. An impressive global web project to be sure, but this does not necessarily lead to reliable information. In fact, there have been numerous cases of blatant errors, politically motivated editing, and a lack of continuity overall. All this said, yes, using Wikipedia as a starting point, and ONLY as a starting point, does have some advantages. Wikipedia can provide a topic overview, key words to springboard research, and links that can be used as reliable resources. But always remember that, as the saying goes, *a chain is only as strong as its weakest link*.

Understanding Available Resources

To save writers from relying on problematic resources, this chapter discusses some of the best resources available to the researcher and how to find them.

Types of Media

Print sources include books, magazines, newspapers, and newsletters (either hard copy or microform). There are reference works like *World Book*, *The Encyclopedia of the Middle Ages*, and *Guide to the Supreme Court*. Print resources are frequently the best places to find background information, even though rigorous research will require sources beyond encyclopedias, almanacs, and atlases.

Non-print resources are videos, films, DVDs, CDs, audiotapes, slides, photographs, and art works. Non-print resources are usually listed in a library's electronic catalogue, and, therefore, more easily accessed.

Electronic resources include computer programs, CD-ROMs, subscription-accessible Internet databases, and Internet websites. Sometimes students have access to a school's subscription database via the media center or password access from any off-campus computer. If there is access, use of subscription sites is highly recommended and is a time saver. Here, editorial control exerted by the producers of the databases assures the validity of these documents and provides more options to tailor a search according to research needs. Electronic resources breakdown into three categories:

> **Subscription Databases** are collections of articles, interviews, transcripts, maps, photos, videos, and many other documents pulled from newspapers, periodicals, reference material, and other sources. Some subscription services also offer original content created by their own writers, which is proprietary and therefore only available to researchers using that particular database. Through these services, information is often immediately available in full text form. ProQuest, CQ Researcher[3] ,and EBSCO[4] are among the most

© 2009. Teacher's Discovery®

popular electronic databases, and many school libraries subscribe as well to GALE[*5], SIRS[*6], and Biography Resource Center[7], databases which create their own original content.

Online Books and Encyclopedias are reference materials found online instead of in physical form. They consist of extensive multimedia materials to supplement subjects and provide a good overview of a topic. Sometimes encyclopedias allow limited free access, but most commonly users are required to have a password to get full access.

Internet Sites vary widely, from authoritative sites like NASA and National Library of Medicine, to sites featuring madmen ranting about the government cover-up of last week's alien invasion. Using the Internet can provide relevant, up-to-date information, but it will also force the researcher to search through millions of documents to find it.

Primary and Secondary Sources

Primary sources are the original words of an individual writer like a speech, an eyewitness report, a personal letter, or remarks in an interview. Further examples in specific fields include these:

The Arts: musical compositions, paintings, films, sculptures, artists' sketchbooks, photography, reproductions, and recordings.

Education: studies, projects, tests and test data, surveys, observations, statistics, and films.

Literature: novels, short stories, essays, poems, autobiographical sketches, diary entries, journal entries, memoirs, and media representations including films, recordings, and performances.

Social Science: agency reports, government records, historical documents, case studies, survey results, the Census, presidential tapes, and market research.

Science: results of experiments and tests; reports of observations and discoveries by those conducting the experiments.

Secondary sources are works about an individual and his/her work, including biographies, histories, critical studies of novels, and discussions of scientific findings. Additional examples include these:

The Arts: reviews and biographies.

Education: articles evaluating educational practices, reports, and books about educational issues and problems.

Literature: articles, reviews, analyses, and books about literary works and writers.

Social science: articles and reports from books, newspapers, and magazines about social issues and historical events.

Science: review and interpretation of scientific experiments, observations, and controversies.

To summarize:
Primary sources are *by the creator of a work*; secondary sources are *about the person and his/her work*.

---

[3] From CQ Press, a division of Sage Publications
[4] EBSCO Information Services, a division of EBSCO Industries, Inc.
[5] Cengage Learning®
[6] ProQuest–CSA LLC
[7] GALE®, a part of Cengage Learning®

© 2009. Teacher's Discovery®

Finding the Right Sources

School Media Center/Library

The school media center/library is the place to start seeking reliable sources. This starts with the trained professional who runs the library. Most school librarians have advanced degrees in Library Science and are specifically trained to help students find the right resources; they know where and how to find the best information quickly and with efficiency. Never hesitate to ask them for help—that's why they are there. It is not unusual to find that the librarians have already selected materials specifically to facilitate student research projects. Furthermore, tapping into the media center's specialized databases first will focus a search in ways the Internet cannot. Looking in books, magazines, reference works, and the like can uncover useful information not found on the Internet. The printing press was invented in the 1500s; the Internet only came along in the 1980s. That's at least 450 years of print that may not have been uploaded yet.

Other Libraries

After a thorough search in the school media center, it's prudent to check out other libraries before searching the Internet. Public and university libraries may have access to broader databases than a secondary school, as well as many more print resources.

The Local Public Library, in town, city, or county, is especially useful when investigating local history. For example, local libraries may have more information about a neighborhood home that was a stop on the Underground Railroad or a local veteran who organized demonstrations against Desert Storm. Some school media centers allow access to the public library catalogue by way of the Web, but utilizing the library staff members and their unique skill set and experience should not be overlooked as an aid. Many libraries are part of a network that loans books back and forth, offering even more possibilities.

The University library, if there is one nearby, is another valuable resource. Although many university libraries restrict circulation privileges to their students and staff, sometimes unregistered individuals can read and photocopy material. College and university library catalogues are accessible on the Internet, and sometimes the media center staff at one school can arrange inter-library loans that give access to another library's materials.

The World Wide Web on the Internet

No doubt, this is a rich field of information, but it requires honed skills to use it effectively. The first stop in starting a research paper shouldn't be Google™. Only after exploring the school's print, non-print, and electronic resources should a student consider a web search. Additionally, before searching the entire Internet, consider searching respected sites that focus on a specific area, or a subject directory that has pre-organized websites by category and subcategory. Appendix B has examples of these tools. After exhausting all aforementioned resources, if additional research is needed, search the Internet. Here are a few tips that will speed that search.

Common Search Tool Terminology

+/-   Use of + (plus) and - (minus) means to include or exclude. For example, *marijuana —medical* retrieves articles about marijuana but omits those devoted to its therapeutic use. Use a space before the sign but not between the sign and the word that follows, e.g., *prejudice +gays* or *prejudice —race*, to focus the search. Note that using + and – gets the same result as using the Boolean operators *and* and *not*, as explained below.

© 2009. Teacher's Discovery®

" " Quotation marks mean that a phrase or concept will be treated as a unit; for example, "*black power*" will get hits about the movement, not display every document that mentions *black* or *power* separately. "*Black power*" +*Stokely Carmichael* will narrow the search further. The search engine will look for an exact match for the phrase in quotation marks.

* Truncation, or shortening a word to its root form, can be an effective search tool when the exact form of the word is not necessary to produce the desired results. By following a search term (keyword) with an asterisk (*), the researcher tells the search engine to automatically include other forms of that word or word root. For example, *Jamaican music** will find Jamaican musicians and musical events, not just music. This function is also called using a wild card or stemming.

and Many searches allow the use of Boolean operators—that is, the connectors *and*, *or*, and *not*—to narrow a search. Using *and* will return hits with both the terms; *or*, with any of the terms; *not* excludes a term. For example, *ice hockey* gets around four million hits. Narrow the search with *ice hockey and injuries, ice hockey and injuries and women*, or *ice hockey and injuries not children*. Some search engines also allow the use of parentheses to avoid confusion in a complicated query. For example, try *opium production and (Afghanistan or Pakistan)*, when searching for results about opium production in either country.

near Some search tools allow the use of the proximity operator *near*. This means the search will return results for a term if it is close to another. For instance, a search using the query *Microsoft and (browser near crash)* will produce results where browser is within a specified number of words from crash. But don't be surprised if that search turns up a few plane crashes.

Language, domain, file type, date, URL, and a variety of other specifications can also limit searches to more manageable results.

Six Tips for Searching the Internet

Tip 1. Use a search engine's help function.

Search engines include tips that are specific to their programs; reading these before beginning a search can make it more effective. For example, under the Google™ help menu, there are sections describing how to use its reference tools as well as special search terminology that can be used to narrow a search.

Tip 2. Choose keywords with care.

They should identify a topic precisely. If necessary, try using synonyms and alternative spellings. For example, "Affirmative Action" and "Racial Quotas" yield quite different results, as do "Agent Orange" and "Effects of Agent Orange."

Tip 3. Review Appendix B: Search Engines.

Review the information in Appendix B; it addresses search engines, subject directories, and meta-search tools, then select the ones best suited for the project. Don't fixate on one search engine or subject directory—different ones can generate different results.

Tip 4. Use advanced searches and power searches.

Remember that most search engines offer advanced or power searches. They also provide a help menu.

© 2009. Teacher's Discovery®

Tip 5. Bookmark websites.

Bookmarking websites, even organizing them by their content, information, or value, makes them easy to find again. Sometimes websites might not appear to have the right information or focus of information; however, later they might come in handy as great secondary references. So be sure they can be found again!

Tip 6. Be smart—avoid plagiarism.

Information on the Internet may not cost money to use, but that doesn't mean it can be used without attribution. As with print sources, anything used in a paper—whether it is summarized, paraphrased, or directly quoted—must be cited properly. It is better to be safe than sorry.

Evaluating Web Sites

Because the information found on the Internet may come from anyone, any place, anytime—from last year's Nobel Laureate in Physics to elementary school children to a detainee of an institution—it is wise to check the reliability of a source. Whether a teacher requires the formal evaluation of resource sites or not, the Website Evaluation Form on page 150 of Appendix A will help ensure that only worthwhile websites are used in the research project.

Authorship: The author of a site needs to be reputable; check his/her credentials. An Ivy League professor, a Nobel Laureate, a renowned poet—these are good signs that the resource is knowledgeable and reputable in his/her respective field. A site or an article without an author should immediately raise a red flag. While some reference material articles do not always include an author, there should always be an organization, university, or other named entity asserting responsibility for the content and the authenticity of the facts, ideas, or information presented.

Sponsorship: The URL can illustrate a great deal about a website's affiliation. URLs with *.edu* and *.gov* mean that they come from an educational or governmental institution. While this does not necessarily mean they are scholarly, it does usually indicate that the information on the site is trustworthy. Reliable information is published and sponsored by a reliable host organization. Any site with a .com, meaning that the sponsor is a commercial (for-profit) organization, should be examined thoroughly.

Currency: It is important to know that the information given is up-to-date and that it is information accepted by some or all of those considered knowledgeable on the subject. The information presented in the website should have a date showing when it was created. In addition, ensure that the website itself continues to be updated and maintained.

Bias: Many authors and organizations have a particular point of view that they are trying to promote. This doesn't necessarily mean their information should not be used; rather, it means that the biases must be noted since they may affect the presentation of the information used. For example, The Heritage Foundation, which produces in-depth analyses of current political policy issues, has a distinctly conservative viewpoint. Likewise, The Center for American Progress, also a producer of in-depth political policy analyses, champions a liberal viewpoint. Not all organizations are as responsible in admitting their biases, so approach any information with a critical eye.

© 2009. Teacher's Discovery®

Using Resources Responsibly— Avoiding Plagiarism

Just as a researcher should be familiar with types of resources and ways he or she can find them, a researcher needs to be aware of how to use these resources appropriately. Plagiarism is viewed as a dishonest act, academic theft; it is every student's responsibility to understand and avoid plagiarizing the works, ideas, and concepts of another individual.

According to the *American Heritage Dictionary of the English Language*, to plagiarize means, "to steal and use (the writings or ideas of another) as one's own."

Note:

Even when it is unintentional, presenting someone else's thoughts, ideas, expressions, or information without proper acknowledgment of the source is an act of academic dishonesty.

After years of being primarily a dirty secret in the academic world, plagiarism has recently been making headlines.

Examples of Celebrity Plagiarism

In 2006 literary sensation Kaavya Viswanathan's novel, *How Opal Mehta Got Kissed, Got Wild, and Got a Life*, was withdrawn and her contract for a second book cancelled when she was discovered to have stolen passages from other authors.

Tim Goeglein, an influential aide to President George W. Bush, resigned his post after admitting to copying material from other articles for his column in the *Fort Wayne News-Sentinel*.

Authors of bestsellers, Alex Haley (*Roots*) and Gail Sheehy (*Passages*), faced lawsuits for failing to document passages apparently lifted from other books.

Well-known historians Stephen Ambrose and Doris Kearns Goodwin had to answer the charge that several paragraphs in their best-selling books bore a close resemblance to those of other authors. The famous writers blamed sloppy scholarship and careless note taking.

Journalist Jayson Blair resigned from *The New York Times* after editors realized that he was systematically plagiarizing other journalists and fabricating facts and sources in his articles.

The consequences in these cases included loss of reputation, dismissals, contract forfeitures, public apologies, and substantial out-of-court settlements.

Plagiarism isn't only a writer's issue. It has undercut musicians as well.

© 2009. Teacher's Discovery®

More Examples

Avril Lavigne is facing a lawsuit from The Rubinoos, who claim that her song "Girlfriend" took lyrics and rhythm from their 1979 song, "I Wanna be Your Boyfriend."

Velvet Revolver was accused of stealing the melody and riff of a song originally by Tony Newton of Voodoo Six, and was ordered to pay him a 20% royalty on sales of their album, as well as all future royalties from the use of that song.

Schools and universities, concerned about academic integrity, are examining their students' works more closely and with aids such as the web-based programs Turnitin˚ (turnitin.com) and EVE2: Essay Verification Engine found at canexus.com.

Examples

In a review of its students' physics papers, the University of Virginia found widespread plagiarism. It led to expulsions and, for some, the revocation of previously awarded degrees.

After conducting an internal investigation, Ohio University discovered engineering students had submitted dozens of plagiarized dissertations.

Secondary school penalties for plagiarism vary in range, but can include these:

Examples

- Receiving a zero for the assignment
- Doing an alternative assignment without possibility of grade improvement
- Parental notification
- Suspension

It is important to note that teachers giving college recommendations usually are required to provide a statement about the student's integrity. Ultimately, one has to ask oneself, "is plagiarism worth it?"

The sale of essays and research papers by Internet paper mills, and the use of so called "study websites" like SparkNotes˚, CliffsNotes (Wiley Publishing, Inc.), and PinkMonkey.com, combined with the ease of cut-and-paste computer features, have contributed to increasing temptation to plagiarize. Rutgers University conducted a study of 23 college campuses. The study revealed that 38% of students admitted to copying up to a paragraph from the Internet without citing the source. What is more disturbing is that somehow the majority of the students willing to admit to plagiarism did not see the behavior as cheating.

The fact is that when someone's words or ideas are borrowed, the source must be cited, or it is plagiarism. The good news is that it is not difficult to avoid plagiarism or its penalties. At the University of Maryland, instructors at the Baltimore County Learning Center have formulated five helpful and simple rules to avoid plagiarism. Janet Graham has granted us permission to distribute these rules with modifications.

Note:

It is important to remember that in a research paper, the teacher will assume that any idea not cited is original to the writer. Whenever using other people's ideas or words, give them credit, whether the source is print or electronic.

© 2009. Teacher's Discovery˚

Avoiding Plagiarism—Five Simple Rules

Rule 1.   A fact that is not common knowledge must have a citation.

Facts that are common knowledge—something that most people in the society would know—can be included without a citation. For example, statements like "The United States desired independence from Great Britain in 1776" need not be cited. Familiar proverbs and sayings such as "Haste makes waste" also do not require citations.

┌─**Example**──

> Scientists have found that the featherless chicken makes as much protein as the feathered chicken
>
> ("Featherless" 43).

Citation needed—not common knowledge
──

Rule 2.   When writing about an idea, make clear whose idea it is.

┌─**Example**──

> After reading several of Fitzgerald's short stories, one can see that Fitzgerald frequently takes the
>
> position of the outsider.

No citation—student's personal observation

> The tone and structure of the poem suggest peace and repose.

No citation—student's personal observation
──

Rule 3.   When writing about someone else's idea, always cite the source.

┌─**Example**──

> By the year 1856, San Francisco's growth was practically certain (Lotchkin 60).

> One might compare Kobe Bryant's downfall to that of Macbeth (Obel A19).
──

Rule 4.   When using someone else's exact words, put those words in quotation marks and always cite the source.

┌─**Example**──

> Later, the author wrote, "Chapter VII (the hotel scene) will never be quite up to mark–I've worried
>
> about it too long and I can't quite place Daisy's reaction" (Fitzgerald 9).

Use a direct quotation only when the author has expressed his or her ideas so perfectly that a paraphrase could not do them justice. (See Rule 5.)
──

© 2009. Teacher's Discovery®

Rule 5. When describing an author's idea, write a description using original wording, not a rearrangement or slight alteration of the author's actual words. Always cite the source.

---Example---

Original:

> "White" ball, then, is the basketball of patience, method and sometimes brute strength. "Black" ball is the basketball of electric self-expression. One player has all the time in the world to perfect his skills, the other a need to prove himself. These are slippery categories, because a poor boy who is black can play "white" and a white boy of middle-class parents can play "black" (Greenfield 215).

Unacceptable Paraphrase:

> "White" ball is playing basketball in a patient, methodical, strong way. "Black" ball is the game of electric self-expression. The white player takes his time to perfect his skills, but the black player wants to prove himself. These categories, however, are slippery. A poor black may play "white," and a middle-class white boy may play "black."

This follows the author's words so closely that it would definitely be considered plagiarism. The student did not use his or her own words to state the idea, nor is the source cited. Both paraphrasing and citation are required.

Acceptable Paraphrase:

The student restates the author's idea in the student's own words and cites the source of the idea. Note that when the author's name—Jeff Greenfield—occurs in the text, the student does not repeat it in the citation but gives only the page. It is not necessary to be repetitive.

> According to Jeff Greenfield, there are fundamental differences between the "white" and the "black" style of basketball. The white player is less hurried; he takes his time, practices his skills systematically, and develops his strength. The black player, on the other hand, proves himself by playing with an almost theatrical flair. Of course, there are exceptions to these categories (215).

© 2009. Teacher's Discovery®

Points to Keep in Mind

To avoid the most common forms of plagiarism, here is a summary of what to keep in mind:

On note cards:

✓ Record notes word for word, whether copying by hand or cutting and pasting from copied or printed material.

✓ Be scrupulous about the accuracy of wording, punctuation, capitalization, and sources. Also, pay attention to the original context and ensure that the recorded notes accurately reflect the original author's intentions.

✓ Don't paraphrase when taking down information; record it exactly. Paraphrase and summarize during the drafting process.

✓ When adding personal comments and observations, distinguish them clearly from copied material. Use a different color ink or enclose the text in brackets.

In the rough draft:

✓ "Cite as you write!" As the first draft is composed, include all citations for borrowed materials. Never leave this until later, thinking to insert sources another time. Trying to find sources after the fact for every citation is tedious. Adding in citations later is also unreliable and can result in unintentional omissions or misplaced citations: plagiarism by accident.

✓ Remember that all borrowed material must be acknowledged, whether it is a direct quote, a paraphrase, or a summary. All information not enclosed in quotation marks must be expressed in the student's own words, and it must include a citation (in parentheses) to the original text. The works cited or reference page, formerly known as the bibliography, should contain the full bibliographic information of the source.

✓ Always go the note card route. Copying material directly into the paper is one of the surest ways to plagiarize.

✓ Downloading Internet documents into a paper is a shortcut to disaster.

In the final version:

✓ Carefully check the entire paper, making sure that all required parenthetical citations are included, that they are accurate, and that they have been punctuated correctly.

✓ Check the works cited or references page for form and accuracy, making sure that the in-text citations correspond to the list of works cited. For example, if (Denby 75) appears in the paper, then the works cited page must include the following entry: Denby, David. *American Sucker*. New York: Little, 2004. Print.

© 2009. Teacher's Discovery®

Three more acts of plagiarism to avoid:

Act 1. **Self-plagiarism**

Submitting a paper that was submitted in a previous class.

Submitting a paper that was previously turned in for another class or another assignment, even if that paper is the student's own work, is considered self-plagiarism. In general, self-plagiarism is not acceptable. There may be situations in which a teacher will accept previously submitted work, but the student must get approval from his/her teacher before turning in the paper.

Act 2. **Procurement plagiarizism**

Getting a research paper in part or in whole from any outside source by way of stealing, purchasing, or copying.

Buying or taking a paper from an Internet site or another student is wrong. Likewise, any student who offers to share papers, journal entries, homework assignments, and the like does a great disservice, both to himself and to his associate. These are acts of academic dishonesty and are likely to incur penalties for both parties. Buying a paper may end up costing a great deal more than the monetary amount paid— personal reputation and future academic standing are at risk.

Act 3. **Collaborative plagiarism**

Working in tandem with another individual or as a group, except where the teacher explicitly permits and encourages cooperation.

Friends, parents, teachers, librarians, and others can be valuable sources of support by offering suggestions about resources, helping to generate ideas, and even proofreading papers, but the research, composition, and revision of the paper is a task for the student alone. For example, the peer editor invited to proofread a paper can indicate when a thesis is unclear or when sentences are awkward, but it is up to the student whose name is on the submitted work to actually revise the thesis and rework the awkward sentence. Unless the instructions specifically allow and/or require group work, then assume that the work required is to be completed by the writer/student alone, and is not the result of undue collaboration with others. When in doubt about what kind of help is allowed, ask.

Because plagiarism has become an increasingly serious problem as students use more and more Internet sources in their research papers, the Modern Language Association has included a chapter on the subject in the seventh edition of the *MLA Handbook*. This chapter is worth a careful reading.[8]

---

[8] A highly entertaining and informative book on this subject is Thomas Mallon, *Stolen Words: The Classic Book on Plagiarism* (New York: Harcourt, 1989).

© 2009. Teacher's Discovery®

Step 1 Summary

- The chief resources for student researchers are the school media center, public and university libraries, and the Internet.

- Libraries offer print, non-print, electronic, and human resources.

- The major electronic resources are information databases, online reference books, and subscription-based online services for various academic disciplines.

- Following a few simple rules will facilitate an Internet search. Consult Appendix B for information about search engines and useful websites.

- Well-known facts and original ideas require no citation. Always cite the source of someone else's ideas, facts, and opinions.

- Using someone else's exact words requires quotation marks and citation of the source.

- Using an author's idea but not quoting it exactly requires a thorough paraphrase, not just a rearrangement of words, and it always includes a citation.

© 2009. Teacher's Discovery®

Step 2
Topic Selection

© 2009. Teacher's Discovery®

Finding a Topic

Having established the best resources available and how to use them properly, it's time to find a topic. In the best of all possible worlds, any topic would be acceptable: marriage between two transgender people, soap operas, skateboarding, the latest Stephanie Meyer novel, or intergalactic travel. Unfortunately, teachers usually impose limitations because they have to follow education standards, course requirements, curriculum objectives, or departmental stipulations. Sometimes teachers assign topics, but more often than not, they distribute a list of acceptable topics from which to choose. If one is lucky, the teacher will include a topic that engages curiosity and sparks interest. Step 2 offers up four tasks that make topic selection easier, and three methods by which to narrow a subject to a manageable scope.

Tasks for Selecting a Topic

Task 1. Select an excellent topic. This means a topic that
- genuinely sparks personal interest.
- is consistent with the purpose of the assignment.
- shows awareness of the intended audience.
- is sufficiently narrow for a project of the length and form assigned.
- has social, historical, political, scientific, or literary significance and/or value.
- is not exceedingly vague or general (for example, the meaning of life, or the causes of world conflict).

Task 2. Find an angle. It's a good idea to
- heed any special requirements for the assignment. Does it call for a position paper, a comparison, a causal analysis, a solution to a problem, or an op-ed piece?
- find an approach that will distinguish this paper from others.
- focus on a specific aspect of the topic instead of trying to deal with a large general subject.
- consult the teacher to confirm that the topic is acceptable. Approval may even be required.

Task 3. Do some serious preliminary work. Serious preliminary work includes
- consulting librarians and other local experts.
- reading articles in general encyclopedias or other reference works.
- making sure that adequate resources are available for the focus being considered.
- using the Internet, databases, and other electronic sources.
- looking at the subject from different angles and taking different approaches. For example:

> **Examples of alternate approaches**
>
> **Koalas**
>
> - Threats to their survival (cause)
> - Differences from bears (comparison, classification)
> - Reasons for their highly specialized diet (cause)

© 2009. Teacher's Discovery®

Global Warming

- Controversy over evidence of recent climate change
- Man-made causes of global warming (cause)
- Natural causes of global warming (cause)
- Dangerous consequences (effect)
- Solutions to the problem

The Battle of Britain

- Differences from other World War II battles (comparison)
- Effect on the outcome of the war (effect)
- Reasons for the Allies' defeat of the Axis (cause, process)

Task 4. Brainstorm. Brainstorming includes

- listing ideas and/or making an outline.
- creating a concept webbing or branching diagram, writing down as many ideas as possible connected with the subject.
- freewriting (also called fastwriting) to generate a flow of ideas on the topic.
- allowing time to contemplate information gathered on the general subject or topics being considered.

Three Methods to Narrow the Subject

Narrowing the subject is one of the most crucial steps in writing a successful research paper. Doing a good job here eliminates wasted time doing in-depth research that later goes unused. The following methods will narrow the focus of a subject into something that can be turned into a thesis statement.

Method 1. Ask questions about the subject.

Turn an intriguing question into a tentative thesis statement. Here are some examples.

Example of general subject and possible questions

The Role of American Women in World War II

Possible research questions:

Why weren't American women drafted into the army?

Of women who enlisted, why were they excluded from combat duty?

What kinds of jobs were available to women in the defense industries?

For what military service could women volunteer?

Did women work as spies, couriers, or cryptographers?

Under what conditions did women pilot aircraft?

How did women aid the war effort?

What were the consequences for women when men came home after the war?

How did World War II influence the women's rights movement?

© 2009. Teacher's Discovery®

Example of a general subject and possible questions

Substance Abuse—Methamphetamine (Crystal Meth)

Possible research questions:

How is crystal meth produced and distributed?

What is the extent of crystal meth usage/abuse, and how and why has it increased?

What are the short-term effects of crystal meth use?

What are the long-term effects of crystal meth use?

Why do children become crystal meth addicts?

What programs are available to help crystal meth addicts?

How can crystal meth use and abuse be prevented?

Method 2. Break the subject into smaller parts.

Take a general subject and look at different, more specific components of the topics that comprise the overall subject. A student considering the subject of social criticism in Charles Dickens's novels might use these strategies:

Concentrate on one novel rather than several. This might yield:

Examples

Dickens's attitude toward the imprisonment of debtors in *David Copperfield.*
or
Dickens's portrayal of child labor in *David Copperfield.*

Focus on a particular problem or aspect:

Examples

Dickens's criticism of the judicial system in *Bleak House.*
or
Dickens's fears about the danger of revolution in *A Tale of Two Cities.*

© 2009. Teacher's Discovery®

Method 3. Simplify a complex subject.

Historical events, such as the Treaty of Versailles and the American Revolution, are so broad and complex that they cannot be dealt with adequately in a single paper. Focus on a specific aspect or take an unusual approach.

Example of ways to simplify a general subject

The Treaty of Versailles

To narrow the subject:

> Prepare diary entries for one of the major participants: Woodrow Wilson, Georges Clemenceau, or Vittorio Emanuele Orlando.

> Debate the validity of a select number of the most important points in Wilson's Fourteen Points.

> Analyze the major problems confronting the treaty negotiators.

> Write an editorial sympathizing with Germany's dissatisfaction with the treaty.

> Assess the consequences of Germany's dissatisfaction.

> Write a speech opposing (or encouraging) American participation in the League of Nations.

Example of ways to simplify a general subject

The American Revolution

Narrow the subject in one of the following ways:

> Compose letters written by one of the leaders of the revolution—John Hancock, Samuel Adams, or Patrick Henry—describing his beliefs and goals in creating a republic.

> Recreate the debate in the Second Continental Congress about whether to declare independence from Britain.

> Write a newspaper article or a pamphlet expressing Loyalist opposition to rebellion and independence.

> Focus on the role of George Washington as Commander-in-Chief of the Continental Army, exploring the military issues and political obstacles he faced.

> Give an eyewitness account of the Battle of Lexington and Concord.

> Discuss the influence of European Enlightenment thinkers such as Rousseau or Locke on Americans such as Thomas Paine.

> Examine the roles of women, African Americans, or Native Americans in the American Revolution.

© 2009. Teacher's Discovery®

Step 2 Summary

A good topic for a research paper is

- narrow enough to be manageable within the assigned length of the paper.

- focused on a single work, issue, theme, or aspect of a bigger subject.

- relevant.

- specific and concrete.

- researchable, not dependent entirely on personal convictions or unavailable resources.

© 2009. Teacher's Discovery®

Step 3

Preliminary Research

Conduct Preliminary Research

Recording Information on Source Cards

© 2009. Teacher's Discovery®

In Step 2, the general subject was examined, preliminary reading was done to get ideas, questions were written about the subject, and finally, a viewpoint was used to narrow the subject to a topic of manageable proportions. Now it is time to start finding the specific resources and information that will be the bricks with which to build the paper.

Conduct Preliminary Research

Keeping the narrowed topic in mind, start searching for books, articles, and other information that will help in the construction of a thesis and provide some of the material necessary to develop points that will support the thesis. Although encyclopedias and general reference sites were consulted in Step 2, more information will be needed before the outlines of a strong paper can take shape. Doing preliminary research now will also ensure that there is enough information available about the chosen topic.

Search the library's electronic catalogue and track down books that are relevant to the topic. Right now, browsing or skimming the text will be enough to gain a better knowledge of the topic and to reveal whether a source is likely to have necessary information. Use the electronic databases and print articles that are likely to be useful. Keep these articles in a safe place; they will be needed in Step 6.

During the preliminary research process, it's a good idea to jot down ideas that seem relevant to the paper. These will come in handy during Step 4: Formulating the Thesis Statement, and Step 5: Making an Outline. When a valuable source is found, it's important to record information about it so that it can easily be retrieved when it's time to start writing note cards.

Recording Information on Source Cards

Source cards are the most convenient way to record the publication information about sources. Although it is not quite time to write note cards, on which one records specific and detailed information to support his or her thesis, it is time to start recording the sources of information found helpful during preliminary research. These sources will provide enough information to develop a tentative thesis statement, and they will reveal some of the main points needed for proving the thesis. In addition, writing source cards now means that there is a record of resources to return to once it is time to start finding specific support for the points that will be recorded on note cards that support the thesis. Finally, the information recorded in the source cards will appear again in the works cited or references page, which is an indispensable part of the research paper that lists the full bibliographic data for every source cited in the paper.

Students with access to the Internet can use handy websites like EasyBib (by ImageEasy Solutions), Landmark's Son of Citation Machine™, or NoodleTools (by Noodles Tools, Inc.). These services help by structuring and punctuating citations accurately. Despite their convenience, however, they are not foolproof. The program cannot generate a correct citation if the student does not enter the correct information about the source being cited. Students often go wrong at the very first step involved in using these programs, when they are asked to choose the type of source that is being cited. If the student cannot correctly identify the source, the computer will ask for inappropriate bibliographic information and then compose an incorrect citation. For example, if a student indicates simply that his/her source is a magazine article, but not that this magazine article was found in an online database instead of a hard copy of the magazine of original publication, the resulting citation will have omitted important and necessary information.

© 2009. Teacher's Discovery®

Additionally, these sites may not be up-to-date with the most recent style specifications. Finally, these services cannot address a source with unusual attributes, since both the APA and MLA styles advise researchers to use individual discretion when dealing with a document that does not fit neatly into prescriptive formats. Consider if it is wiser to handwrite or type out the source cards rather than rely on possibly faulty technological tools.

Because citations provide both a record of the research done and credit to the original authors, it is imperative that citations be faultless. Whichever citation method is used, refer to this guide or the most recent MLA or APA style guidelines to confirm all source card citations are complete.

Study the diagram of model source cards that follow. Note the information provided and its arrangement, or format. Carefully read through the tasks of the process.

Source Card Diagrams

MLA Book Format   ### APA Book Format

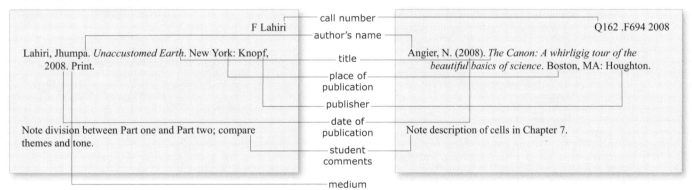

MLA Article from a Database Format   ### APA Article from a Database Format

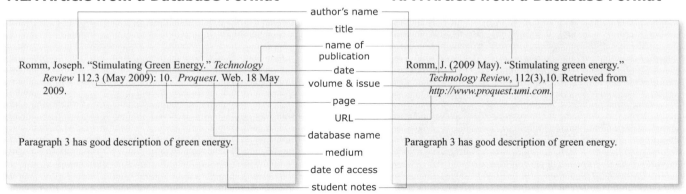

© 2009. Teacher's Discovery®

Procedure for Writing Source Cards

Task 1. Review

Review Step 1, which discusses the resources available for research.

Notice the great variety of sources of information now found in computerized catalogues: books, magazines, videos, CDs, DVDs, microfilm, reference works, etc. There are electronic sources too numerous to list that include online databases, newspaper indexes, and CD-ROM programs.

If the school librarian provides orientation for specific research projects, listen carefully; it will eliminate hours of fruitless searching.

Task 2. Supplies

When a potential information source is located, use a pen and lined 3 x 5-inch index cards (source cards) to record the information. Some teachers may allow students to compose source cards on the computer in a word processing program. Either way, put the source information in exactly the format that will be needed later for the works cited or reference page. Study the models before writing the card, and check them later for accuracy. Notice that the correct format for source cards and for entries on the works cited or reference page is the same.

Some databases provide citations at the end of articles. While this can be helpful, always double check the format with the most recent MLA or APA guidelines.

Task 3. MLA Formatting

Record the following information on each card. For each entry, indent the second line and subsequent lines of the entry five spaces or one-half inch. Look at the examples at the end of this chapter to see the exact format of each entry.

a. Call number, if available, in upper right corner.

b. Author's full name, last name first; include middle initial if used.

c. Title of book, in italics (or underlined, if written by hand); or title of article, in quotation marks. Separate the title from the subtitle (if there is one) with a colon.

d. For a **book**: place of publication—that is, the city listed on the title or copyright page (no state or country); the publisher, in short form; date of publication, usually the same as the copyright date; and medium (Print). If several cities are given, use only the first one, and use only the latest date given.

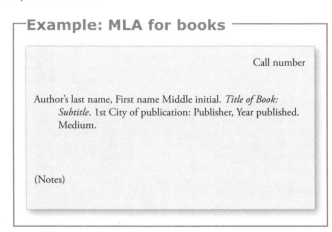

Example: MLA for books

Call number

Author's last name, First name Middle initial. *Title of Book: Subtitle*. 1st City of publication: Publisher, Year published. Medium.

(Notes)

© 2009. Teacher's Discovery®

e. For an **article** in a periodical, such as a magazine, newspaper, or scholarly journal, include also the following information: series number (if relevant); volume number (not necessary for magazines or newspapers); issue number (not necessary for magazines or newspapers); date; pages; and medium (Print). Consult the model for order, capitalization, and punctuation. If a periodical is found in an online database, add to the above information: name of the database (italicized), medium (Web), and date of access.

⌐Example: MLA for an article in a periodical

Call number

Author's last name, First name Middle initial. "Title of Article: Subtitle." *Title of Periodical* Volume number.issue number (day Month year): pages. Medium.

(Notes)

f. For **web pages:** author; title of the work (italicized if the work is independent; in quotation marks if the work is part of a larger work); title of the overall website; version or edition; site publisher or sponsor (if not available, use N.p.; publication date (if nothing is available, use n.d.); medium of publication (Web); and date of access, including day, month, and year.

⌐Example: MLA for a web page

Call number

Author's last name, First name, Middle initial. "Title of Web Page." *Title of the Overall Website*. Version/Edition. Publisher or sponsor, day Month year. Medium. day Month year of access.

(Notes)

g. For **a work found on the Web that is also available in print format,** include all the appropriate print information and then add title of the database or website (italicized); medium of publication (Web); and date of access.

h. For other source types, such as letters, films, artwork, etc., see the formatting examples in Step 10, pages 125-133.

⌐Example: MLA for a work found on the Web that is also available in print

Call number

Author's last name, first name Middle initial. *Title of Work*. City of publication: Publisher, Year published. *Title of Website*. Medium. day Month year of access.

(Notes)

Examples: MLA source cards (handwritten)

Note that the following examples are of handwritten source cards showing the titles as underlined. If these were typed or computer generated source cards, the underlined titles would be italicized instead.

Article in a Reference Book

"Prehistory and the Great Ice Age." The Encyclopedia of World History. Ed. Peter Stearns. 6th ed. New York: Houghton, 2002. Print.

Book with a translator

Beowulf. Trans. Seamus Heaney. New York: Norton, 2001. Print.

Essay in an anthology

YA Fic-Firebirds

Springer, Nancy. "Mariposa." Firebirds: An Anthology of Original Fantasy and Science Fiction. Ed. Sharyn November. New York: Penguin, 2005. 107-121. Print.

Online book

Carroll, Lewis. Alice's Adventures in Wonderland. New York: Appleton, 1866. University of Virginia E-text Center. Web. 13 May 2009.

Article in a magazine

Hayes, Stephen F. "The Long Road Back: A Texas Bicycle Ride helps Wounded Veterans Rehabilitate and Reconnect." The Weekly Standard 27 Apr. 2009: 16-24. Print

Film on DVD

The Merchant of Venice. Dir. Michael Radford. Perf. Al Pacino, Jeremy Irons. DVD. MGM, 2004.

Note specific ways the movie differs from the play.

Task 3. APA Formatting

Record the following information on each card. For each entry, indent the second line and subsequent lines of the entry five spaces or one-half inch. Look at the examples at the end of this chapter to see the exact form of each entry.

a. Call number, if available, in upper right corner.

b. Author's surname first; use initials for first and middle names.

c. Publication date, in parentheses (year, month, day).

© 2009. Teacher's Discovery®

d. Title of book, in italics (or underlined, if written by hand); or title of article, not underlined or in quotation marks. Capitalize as follows: capitalize the first word, the first word after a dash or colon, and proper nouns. Do not capitalize the second word of a hyphenated compound word (for example, After-shock).

e. For a **book**, place of publication—that is, the city and state for U.S. publishers; add the country for publishers outside the United States. Use the official two-letter U.S. Postal Service abbreviations for states. List the publisher, omitting Publishers, Co., or Inc. but retaining Books and Press.

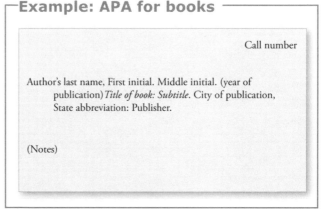

Example: APA for books

Call number

Author's last name, First initial. Middle initial. (year of publication) *Title of book: Subtitle*. City of publication, State abbreviation: Publisher.

(Notes)

f. For an **article in a periodical, magazine**, or **newspaper**, include the volume number, in italics, and the issue number and pages, not italicized, in Arabic numerals. Consult the model for order, capitalization, punctuation, and additional details.

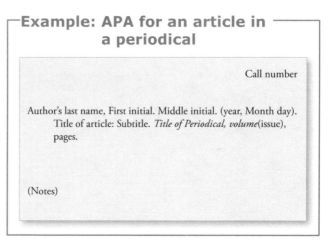

Example: APA for an article in a periodical

Call number

Author's last name, First initial. Middle initial. (year, Month day). Title of article: Subtitle. *Title of Periodical, volume*(issue), pages.

(Notes)

g. For **electronic sources**, follow the specifications for print sources but include the digital object identification (DOI*) number, if available. This number can be found on the first page of the article, near the copyright notice, or in the document details or indexing function. If the article does not have a DOI number, write "Retrieved from" and then cite the home page URL of the database or publisher. If the article or webpage would be difficult to find from the home page, include the full URL address.

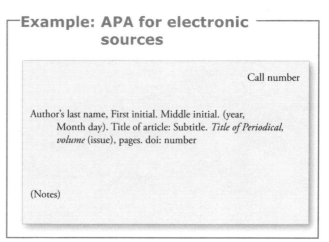

Example: APA for electronic sources

Call number

Author's last name, First initial. Middle initial. (year, Month day). Title of article: Subtitle. *Title of Periodical, volume* (issue), pages. doi: number

(Notes)

h. For other source types, such as letters, films, artwork, etc, see the formatting examples in Step 10, pages 137-141.

© 2009. Teacher's Discovery®

Examples: APA source cards (handwritten)

Note that the following examples are of handwritten source cards showing the titles as underlined. If these were typed or computer generated source cards, the underlined titles would be italicized instead.

Book

579.342 Zun

Zimmer, K. (2008). <u>Microcosm: E. coli and the new science</u> of life. Toronto, ON CAN: Pantheon.

Website

Hitt, D. (2009, May 5). STS-125: Mission to Hubble. Retrieved from http://www.nasa/gov.audience/foreducators/sts125-mission-to-hubble.html

Article in a magazine

Ashley, S. (2003, October). Artificial muscles. <u>Scientific American</u>, 289, 52-59.

Scholarly journal article from online database

Johnson, M.K., Crosnoe, R., & Thadden, L. (2006, September). Gendered patterns in adolescents' school attachment. <u>Social Psychology Quarterly</u>,69, 284-295. Retrieved from http://www.jstor.org/stable/20141746

DVD

American Psychological Association. (Producer). (2009). <u>Parenting young children</u> [DVD]. Available from http://www/apa.org/videos

Audio recording

Westen, D. (1998). The psychoanalytic theory of conflict. Lecture 4 in <u>Is anyone really normal? Perspectives on abnormal psychology</u>. [Cassette recording]. Chantilly, VA: Teaching Company.

Compare to other conflict theories.

© 2009. Teacher's Discovery®

Task 4. Notes

Add personal critical comments, suggestions, or reminders, either at the bottom of the card or on the back. Although most teachers make this step optional, it's useful to jot down the numbers of pages, chapters, or sections that look promising.

Task 5. Grading

Some teachers require that source cards be turned in for review. Teachers expect the cards to contain complete information in the correct format, and this includes spelling, punctuation, and capitalization.

Task 6. Address errors

If teacher returns the cards with comments or errors noted, make the necessary corrections immediately. Keep source cards in a safe place. Small sealable plastic bags are useful for carrying cards and storing them. When using a word processing program, save often and consider keeping a printed copy of the latest version.

Upon completion of the final written paper, alphabetize the source cards actually used and prepare the works cited page, using the information on the cards. Consult Step 10: Works Cited Page, and note the model provided.

© 2009. Teacher's Discovery®

Step 3 Summary

Source cards

- record publication information required for accurate documentation.

- match the exact formatting for entries on the works cited or references page.

- are recorded on 3 x 5-inch lined index cards.

- require specific information in proper form.

© 2009. Teacher's Discovery®

Step 4

Formulate a Thesis Statement

© 2009. Teacher's Discovery®

Approaching the Thesis Statement

The thesis statement is one of the most important parts of the research paper. It asserts the main point of the paper and clarifies the scope of the topic that will be addressed. Because it states the purpose of the paper, or what the writer is trying to prove, the thesis statement appears at the beginning of the paper, usually in the first paragraph.

There are several approaches to selecting a thesis statement. Teachers may provide each student with a thesis statement; teachers may ask that the thesis statement be limited to those on a predetermined list; or teachers may allow students the freedom to choose their own thesis statements, with or without supervision or assistance. This chapter deals with the latter, when the thesis statement is an original idea unique to the individual student.

Arriving at a Satisfactory Thesis Statement

It is likely that the preliminary research has allowed for some insight into the chosen topic. Now it is time to construct a tentative thesis statement. The following tasks and examples illustrate this process.

Task 1.   Propose a judgment, criticism, or evaluation that can be supported in a paper of the prescribed length. This is a temporary, tentative thesis statement that will be refined later.

Task 2.   Determine how to back up the thesis statement by deciding what source material supports the judgment, criticism, or evaluation. What information provides evidence, reasons, and arguments to convince a reader that the thesis statement is sound?

© 2009. Teacher's Discovery®

A good thesis statement

is a declarative sentence stating clearly and concisely the author's main point.

---Example---

The perceived injustices of the Treaty of Versailles made it a major cause of World War II.

---

is a sentence embodying a judgment, evaluation, or criticism, and is apparent in its use of value terms, e.g., *good, better, best, valuable, worthwhile, desirable, favorable, major, most important, effective, significant, insightful,* or *should.*

---Example---

The major obstacles that made the Treaty of Versailles difficult to enforce concerned disarmament, reparations, and the punishment of war criminals.

---

is a statement that can be considered significant because it contributes to scholarly understanding of a subject. A thesis statement should indicate to the reader that the author has something worth saying.

---Example---

Instead of the thesis, "Playing video games is fun," develop a more significant idea about video games, like "Video games are an important developmental tool for young people because they enhance eye-hand coordination, develop complex problem-solving skills, and promote self-confidence."

---

may suggest a comparison or a contrast.

---Example---

The treaty that followed World War II was radically different from the one that concluded World War I.

---

may focus primarily on the causes or effects of a particular event, condition, or change.

---Example---

A number of economic and political developments in Europe made World War I almost inevitable.

---

may propose a solution to a problem or recommend a policy.

---Example---

Community service should be mandatory for all high school students, and should take place during the school hours.

© 2009. Teacher's Discovery®

A good thesis statement

 is not a statement of fact.

┌─**Example**───────────────────────────────────────┐

Statement of fact	**Thesis statement**
The Treaty of Versailles was signed by the four major powers and became effective January 1920.	The competing national interests of the four major powers who negotiated the Treaty of Versailles led to some deeply problematic provisions.

└──┘

 is not merely the expression of a personal opinion.

┌─**Example**───────────────────────────────────────┐

Purely a personal opinion	**Thesis statement**
I think the Treaty of Versailles was a foolish mistake.	The severe punishments, loss of territory, and steep reparation payments required by the Treaty of Versailles created turmoil in Germany, which later spread to the rest of Europe.

└──┘

 is not a generalization.

┌─**Example**───────────────────────────────────────┐

Generalization	**Thesis statement**
The Treaty of Versailles caused the world a lot of problems.	German resentment toward the war-guilt clause in the Treaty of Versailles directly contributed to the rise of Adolph Hitler.

└──┘

 is not written in the form of a question.

┌─**Example**───────────────────────────────────────┐

Question	**Thesis statement**
Was the Treaty of Versailles a major force in precipitating World War II?	The Treaty of Versailles was a major force in precipitating World War II.

└──┘

© 2009. Teacher's Discovery®

Good Thesis Statements

The examples below show how a writer moves from general subject to narrowed topic to precise thesis statement.

Example A

General subject: Genocide in Darfur

Specific topic: Humanitarian help for refugees

Thesis statement: The policies of the Sudanese government toward humanitarian groups hinder attempts by aid workers to help fleeing refugees of ethnic violence in Darfur.

Example B

General subject: History of the Jewish people

Specific topic: The attempt to establish a Jewish homeland

Thesis statement: American Zionists played an important role in the struggle to establish a Jewish homeland.

Example C

General subject: Marriage equality

Specific topic: Arguments opposing the legalization of same-sex marriage

Thesis statement: Within the Judeo-Christian tradition, there are strong religious beliefs against extending the definition of marriage to include same-sex couples.

Example D

General subject: Video game design

Specific topic: Use of math in the creation of video games

Thesis statement: Understanding mathematical principles is important for video game creators, who use tangents and parametric equations to control movement and create realistic playing scenarios.

© 2009. Teacher's Discovery®

Step 4 Summary

An excellent thesis statement is

- a judgment, criticism, or evaluation that research supports.

- a declarative sentence that states the main point of the essay.

- interesting and provides a significant contribution to scholarship.

- NOT a factual statement, not expressed as a personal opinion, not a generalization, and not written as a question.

© 2009. Teacher's Discovery®

Step 5

Making an Outline

Determine the Major Supporting Topics

Creating the Outline

© 2009. Teacher's Discovery®

Determine the Major Supporting Topics

Once the thesis statement is formulated, it is time to tackle Part A of creating an outline: finding topics to support the thesis. Do this before the note-taking process, when specific information is recorded on note cards. Figuring out how to support the thesis statement will help to identify useful topic headings for the note cards, to distinguish between relevant and irrelevant material, and to know where to put that relevant material. A coherent rough draft requires systematic note taking based on a solid starting outline.

Procedure

After narrowing the subject and drafting a tentative thesis statement, divide the narrowed topic into three or more major supporting topics to provide support for the thesis—that is, evidence or arguments that will convince the reader that the thesis is valid.

Example

To support the thesis statement that dogs have been useful to mankind throughout history, Chris first listed some ways that dogs have served humans:

> Hunting and tracking
> Guarding and attacking
> Sniffing out drugs or bombs
> Acting as guide dogs for the blind
> Providing companionship
> Pulling sleds in snowy regions
> Finding victims in collapsed buildings
> Herding sheep and other farm animals

From these, she selected the three ways that she found most interesting. She made sure they were promising as major topics—that is, topics about which she expected to find plenty of information to provide examples, details, facts, statistics, and excellent quotations. She chose:

> A. Hunting
> B. Guiding
> C. Providing companionship

As she did her research and note taking, she found another promising topic, which she added as a subtopic to B: aiding the deaf by recognizing sounds like the doorbell or phone. Notice that topics A, B, and C all support Chris's thesis statement: they provide reasons or arguments for accepting it.

© 2009. Teacher's Discovery®

Recall that these supporting arguments are called the **Method of Development (MOD)**. As further examples, here are several student thesis statements and topics that support them.

Examples: thesis statement and MOD

Women's basketball has changed radically since the game was introduced at Smith College in 1892.

    A. Court size and restricted playing areas

    B. Limitations on running, dribbling, and reaching in

    C. Other rules of the game

    D. Players' clothing

Dolphins are highly intelligent creatures that share several abilities with humans.

    A. Imitation, memorization

    B. Foresight, learning from observation, communicating experience

    C. Solving complex problems, performing elaborate tasks

The dramatic increase of childhood obesity in the United States is a result of modern lifestyles.

    A. TV and video games as leisure activities

    B. Availability of processed foods high in fat and calories

    C. Others: Dependence on cars? Less time for exercise? Junk food advertising aimed at children?

There seem to be some negative, long-term consequences of marijuana smoking, but the evidence is inconclusive.

    A. Alteration of attention

    B. Memory impairment

    C. Physical addiction

    D. Increased risk of lung cancer

Loneliness and alienation are dominant themes in the fiction of J. D. Salinger.

    A. Isolation from family

    B. Isolation from individuals

    C. Isolation from society and institutions

Although they tell the same story, William Shakespeare's play *Romeo and Juliet* and Baz Luhrman's film version of the same name differ in several important ways.

    A. Length and complexity

    B. Setting

    C. Dramatic impact

    D. Dialogue

Cheating has been part of professional baseball in the United States since the first game was played in 1871.

    A. Tampering with equipment

    B. Dishonest groundskeeping

    C. Using illegal devices to steal signals

© 2009. Teacher's Discovery®

Creating the Outline

The outline is an important component of the research process that will help provide focus and clarity in the final product. The key points about an outline are these:

- it provides the **structure** for the paper.

- it makes **relationships** among main ideas and supporting facts visible.

- it **changes**. Keep revising the outline as research and writing progress so it reflects new insights, deletions, modifications, connections, and improvements.

- it is finished only when the final paper is finished. Only then can it be written in stone.

Preliminary Topic Outline

Now, take a look at this sample outline below. It is the skeleton to be filled in as research continues. Each major supporting topic will have examples and details specific to itself. There may be two or more examples for each supporting topic.

Example Preliminary Outline A

Thesis Statement A.

A. First Major Supporting Topic
1. Specific examples, details
2. Specific examples, details
3. Specific examples, details

B. Second Major Supporting Topic
1. Specific examples, details
2. Specific examples, details
3. Specific examples, details

C. Third Major Supporting Topic
1. Specific examples, details
2. Specific examples, details
3. Specific examples, details

Example Preliminary Outline B

Thesis Statement B.

A. First Major Supporting Topic
1. Subtopic
a. Specific examples, details
b. Specific examples, details

2. Subtopic
a. Specific examples, details
b. Specific examples, details

B. Second Major Supporting Topic
1. Specific examples, details
2. Specific examples, details

C. Third Major Supporting Topic
1. Specific examples, details
2. Specific examples, details

© 2009. Teacher's Discovery®

Here's an example of the way one student formulated a thesis statement and determined the major supporting topics.

Example

First, Jon wrote a tentative thesis statement about the dangers of professional football.

Then, based on his knowledge of the sport and on some preliminary reading, he decided to try these supporting topics:

    A. Head injuries

    B. Shoulder and spinal cord injuries

    C. Knee injuries, leg fractures

Finally, he wrote down his thesis statement and entered his major supporting topics on the outline opposite A, B, and C.

Later, after doing his research, he filled in a brief list of examples, facts, quotations, and the like that he would use in his paper. He entered them under each major supporting topic, using the numbers provided.

During his research, he also found another major supporting topic.

    D. Injuries resulting from artificial turf

Of course, Jon may end up finding so much information about head injuries that he will decide to limit his essay just to concussions suffered by quarterbacks. In that case, he'll change his thesis statement and revise his major supporting topics. Since writing a research paper is an exploration, it's not surprising that the writer/researcher's path often ends up in an unexpected place.

This is what Jon's preliminary outline looks like:

Example

Thesis statement: Despite efforts to improve safety through rules and equipment changes, professional football is a violent game that causes many serious injuries.

    A. Head injuries [major supporting topic and heading on note cards.]
        1. Statistical or numerical evidence the incidence of head injuries in the National Football League.
        2. Quotation from Dr. Robert Cantu, medical director of the National Center for Catastrophic Sports Injury Research in Chapel Hill, NC.
        3. Example: Ben Roethlisberger, Pittsburgh Steelers quarterback, who has suffered multiple concussions.

    B. Shoulder and spinal cord injuries [major supporting topic and heading on note cards]
        1.
        2.
        3.

    C. Knee injuries [major supporting topic and heading on note cards]
        1.
        2.
        3.

© 2009. Teacher's Discovery®

Points to Remember

Point 1. Look for examples, facts, statistics, details, and quotations within the major supporting topics. Preliminary research may have already yielded some of the specifics needed, but in most cases the outline will guide the researcher to the information that needs to be recorded on note cards to support the major topics. In this case, Jon will conduct research efficiently by focusing his efforts on finding details for these topics:

> **Examples**
>
> A. Head injuries
> B. Shoulder and spinal cord injuries
> C. Knee injuries

Point 2. Remember that the major supporting topics are also the headings that will be written at the top of the note cards, which will be discussed in more detail in Step 6. The preliminary outline may reveal that major supporting topics should be divided into subtopics, which would also be reflected in the note card headings. For example, head injuries might subdivide into *injuries to quarterbacks* and *injuries to other players*.

> **Examples**
>
> A. Head injuries
>   1. injuries to quarterbacks
>   2. injuries to other players
> B. Shoulder and spinal cord injuries
> C. Knee injuries

Point 3. The number of major supporting topics needed is not fixed, but two is the minimum, and three or more are common. Add another major supporting topic or subdivision if needed.

Point 4. The number of supporting subtopics is also not fixed, but it shouldn't be less than two under a given major supporting topic. Under **Head** injuries, for example, there could be information about concussions suffered by quarterbacks Trent Green, Kurt Warner, Joe Montana, Steve Young, and Troy Aikman. These topics each support the claim that football is dangerous.

Point 5. Strive for logic, consistency, and completeness in the outline. Make lettering and indenting reflect the logical relationship among the ideas: the major supporting topics are the chief proof for the thesis statement, and the supporting subtopics and example/details provide further proof in the form of facts, quotations, statistics, and examples.

Point 6. The preliminary outline is a barebones, tentative indication of how the paper will shape up and, as such, does not need to include full sentences. Check with the teacher to be sure. The final outline reflects the changes that occurred in thinking as research progressed, and reflects the exact structure of the final product. See Appendix A, pages 151-152, for examples of outline formats for two types of research papers.

© 2009. Teacher's Discovery®

Step 5 Summary

To find the major supporting topics for the thesis statement:

- write down the tentative thesis statement.

- list as many supporting topics as knowledge allows.

- select the three or four most promising major supporting topics.

- do preliminary reading to locate supporting information for the major supporting topics.

- add or drop major topics as research progresses.

Outlines

- make clear the structure of the paper.

- show how supporting topics and supporting subtopics connect to the thesis statement.

- reflect the headings on the note cards as the major supporting topics in the outline.

- will change during the research process.

© 2009. Teacher's Discovery®

Step 6

Taking Notes

Targeting Useful Information

Using Relevant Material

Composing Note Cards

© 2009. Teacher's Discovery®

In this step we'll address note taking, one of the most time-consuming tasks in the research paper process. Keep in mind this cardinal rule:

The quality of the notes taken is more important than the quantity.

It is necessary to practice note-taking skills before one can write a successful research paper.

Reviewing the Process to Date:

- The subject has been selected. (Pages 22-26)

- The tentative thesis statement has been formulated. (Pages 38-42)

- Sources have been located. (Page 28)

- Source cards have been made. (Pages 28-35)

- The topic outline has been created, showing at least three major supporting topics as evidence for the thesis statement. (Pages 44-49)

Now, there are printed pages to the left and a pile of blank note cards to the right. What to do next? Here's an example that will show how to proceed and offer opportunity to practice.

Targeting Useful Material

Finding material that will support the thesis is one of the most important parts of the research process. This section explains how to go about this task by focusing on one student and his technique for selecting relevant material from an article he found during the preliminary research stage.

This is Mark's tentative thesis statement:

Teenagers' excessive consumption of alcohol may cause serious damage to both mind and body.

From his preliminary reading, Mark decided to support his thesis statement with the following two major supporting topics:

1. **Short-term effects**—that is, those evident during and immediately following drinking

2. **Long-term effects**, divided into the supporting subtopics:
   a. Physical effects—i.e., effects on the body
   b. Psychological effects—i.e., effects on the mind and behavior

He planned to concentrate mainly on long-term effects, since they struck him as the most serious, but he also wanted to include such short-term consequences as passing out, vomiting, and hangovers. Because these may be more familiar to his audience, Mark figured they might provide a good lead-in for his main discussion.

Mark's next step was to read carefully an article that looked promising. While doing preliminary research for Step 3, Mark had searched the National Institute of Health's website, which included reports submitted by the National Institute of Alcoholism and Alcohol Abuse. He had printed a copy of a report entitled "Why Do Adolescents Drink, What Are the Risks, and How Can Underage Drinking Be Prevented?", knowing that the description of alcohol's effects on teenagers would be valuable when he was ready to start taking notes.

Mark is now ready to annotate, that is to say, underline and make marginal notes. Because he has a printed copy of the article, he can write directly on the paper. Many students like to use a highlighter for this step because highlighting makes it easier to pick out relevant information later.

Observe Mark's approach to this article as an example of how to target and record useful information.

Mark's Technique for Targeting Useful Information

Task 1. First, Mark read the article, "Why Do Adolescents Drink, What Are the Risks, and How Can Underage Drinking Be Prevented?"

As he read, he wrote notes on the article, remembering that his thesis, or the purpose of his paper, was to prove that teenagers' consumption of alcohol could cause serious damage to their minds and bodies. He specifically looked for short-term and long-term effects, and for effects on both body and mind, as it pertains to teens, since those were the topics he had determined would support his thesis statement. He ignored other information and details not immediately relevant to these topics.

He used these headings to identify relevant information:

ST for short-term effects

LT for long-term effects

Phys. for physical effects

Psych. for psychological effects

Notice that Mark has identified only those paragraphs that contain information about the effects of teenage drinking. He ignored other material in the article, knowing that his note taking must be highly selective. He takes down only what specifically supports his thesis statement.

© 2009. Teacher's Discovery®

UNDERAGE DRINKING

*Why Do Adolescents Drink,
What Are the Risks, and How Can
Underage Drinking Be Prevented?*

1 Alcohol is the drug of choice among youth. Many young people are experiencing the consequences of drinking too much, at too early an age. As a result, underage drinking is a leading public health problem in this country.

LT phys.— death

ST phys.— injuries

2 Each year, approximately 5,000 young people under the age of 21 die as a result of underage drinking; this includes about 1,900 deaths from motor vehicle crashes, 1,600 as a result of homicides, 300 from suicide, as well as hundreds from other injuries such as falls, burns, and drownings (1–5).

3 Yet drinking continues to be widespread among adolescents, as shown by nationwide surveys as well as studies in smaller populations. According to data from the 2005 Monitoring the Future (MTF) study, an annual survey of U.S. youth, three-fourths of 12th graders, more than two-thirds of 10th graders, and about two in every five 8th graders have consumed alcohol. And when youth drink they tend to drink intensively, often consuming four to five drinks at one time. MTF data show that 11 percent of 8th graders, 22 percent of 10th graders, and 29 percent of 12th graders had engaged in heavy episodic (or "binge[1]") drinking within the past two weeks (6) (see figure).

4 Research also shows that many adolescents start to drink at very young ages. In 2003, the average age of first use of alcohol was about 14, compared to about 17 1/2 in 1965 (7,8). People who reported starting to drink before the age of 15 were four times more likely to also report meeting the criteria for alcohol dependence at some point in their lives (9). In fact, new research shows that the serious drinking problems (including what is called alcoholism) typically associated with middle age actually begin to appear much earlier, during young adulthood and even adolescence.

LT Pysch.— danger of alcoholism

5 Other research shows that the younger children and adolescents are when they start to drink, the more likely they will be to engage in behaviors that harm themselves and others. For example, frequent binge drinkers (nearly 1 million high school students nationwide) are more likely to engage in risky behaviors, including using other drugs such as marijuana and cocaine, having sex with six or more partners, and earning grades that are mostly Ds and Fs in school (10).

LT Pysch.— risky behavior

[1] The National Institute on Alcohol Abuse and Alcoholism (NIAAA) defines binge drinking as a pattern of drinking alcohol that brings blood alcohol concentration (BAC) to 0.08 grams per cent or above. For the typical adult, this pattern corresponds to consuming five or more drinks (men), or four or more drinks (women), in about 2 hours.

WHY DO SOME ADOLESCENTS DRINK?

6 As children move from adolescence to young adulthood, they encounter dramatic physical, emotional, and lifestyle changes. Developmental transitions, such as puberty and increasing independence, have been associated with alcohol use. So in a sense, just being an adolescent may be a key risk factor not only for starting to drink but also for drinking dangerously.

7 *Risk-Taking*—Research shows the brain keeps developing well into the twenties, during which time it continues to establish important communication connections and further refines its function. Scientists believe that this lengthy developmental period may help explain some of the behavior which is characteristic of adolescence—such as their propensity to seek out new and potentially dangerous situations. For some teens, thrill-seeking might include experimenting with alcohol.

8 *Expectancies*—How people view alcohol and its effects also influences their drinking behavior, including whether they begin to drink and how much. An adolescent who expects drinking to be a pleasurable experience is more likely to drink than one who does not. An important area of alcohol research is focusing on how expectancy influences drinking patterns from childhood through adolescence and into young adulthood (11–14). Beliefs about alcohol are established very early in life, even before the child begins elementary school (15). Before age 9, children generally view alcohol negatively and see drinking as bad, with adverse effects. By about age 13, however, their expectancies shift, becoming more positive (11,16).

9 *Sensitivity and Tolerance to Alcohol*—Differences between the adult brain and the brain of the maturing adolescent also may help to explain why many young drinkers are able to consume much larger amounts of alcohol than adults (17) before experiencing the negative consequences of drinking, such as drowsiness, lack of coordination, and withdrawal/ hangover effects (18,19). This unusual tolerance may help to explain the high rates of binge drinking among young adults. At the same time, adolescents appear to be particularly sensitive to the positive effects of drinking, such as feeling more at ease in social situations, and young people may drink more than adults because of these positive social experiences (18,19).

ST phys.— drowsiness, lack of coordination, hangover

10 *Personality Characteristics and Psychiatric Comorbidity*—Children who begin to drink at a very early age (before age 12) often share similar personality characteristics that may make them more likely to start drinking. Young people who

© 2009. Teacher's Discovery®

are disruptive, hyperactive, and aggressive—often referred to as having conduct problems or being antisocial—as well as those who are depressed, withdrawn, or anxious, may be at greatest risk for alcohol problems (20). Other behavior problems associated with alcohol use include rebelliousness (21), difficulty avoiding harm or harmful situations (22), and a host of other traits seen in young people who act out without regard for rules or the feelings of others (i.e., disinhibition) (23–25).

11 *Hereditary Factors*—Some of the behavioral and physiological factors that converge to increase or decrease a person's risk for alcohol problems, including tolerance to alcohol's effects, may be directly linked to genetics. For example, being a child of an alcoholic or having several alcoholic family members places a person at greater risk for alcohol problems. Children of alcoholics (COAs) are between 4 and 10 times more likely to become alcoholics themselves than are children who have no close relatives with alcoholism (26).

12 *Environmental Aspects*—Pinpointing a genetic contribution will not tell the whole story, however, as drinking behavior reflects a complex interplay between inherited and environmental factors, the implications of which are only beginning to be explored in adolescents (43). And what influences drinking at one age may not have the same impact at another. As Rose and colleagues (43) show, genetic factors appear to have more influence on adolescent drinking behavior in late adolescence than in mid-adolescence.

13 Environmental factors, such as the influence of parents and peers, also play a role in alcohol use (44). For example, parents who drink more and who view drinking favorably may have children who drink more, and an adolescent girl with an older or adult boyfriend is more likely to use alcohol and other drugs and to engage in delinquent behaviors (45).

WHAT ARE THE HEALTH RISKS?

14 Whatever it is that leads adolescents to begin drinking, once they start they face a number of potential health risks. Although the severe health problems associated with harmful alcohol use are not as common in adolescents as they are in adults, studies show that young people who drink heavily may put themselves at risk for a range of potential health problems.

15 *Brain Effects*—Scientists currently are examining just how alcohol affects the developing brain, but it's a difficult task. Subtle changes in the brain may be difficult to detect but still have a significant impact on long-term thinking and memory skills. Add to this the fact that adolescent brains are still maturing, and the study of alcohol's effects becomes even more complex. Research has shown that animals fed alcohol during this critical

LT psych.— possible impairment of long-term memory and learning skills

developmental stage continue to show long-lasting impairment from alcohol as they age (47). It's simply not known how alcohol will affect the long-term memory and learning skills of people who began drinking heavily as adolescents.

16 *Liver Effects*—Elevated liver enzymes, indicating some degree of liver damage, have been found in some adolescents who drink alcohol (48). Young drinkers who are overweight or obese showed elevated liver enzymes even with only moderate levels of drinking (49).

LT phys.— liver damage

17 *Growth and Endocrine Effects*—In both males and females, puberty is a period associated with marked hormonal changes, including increases in the sex hormones, estrogen and testosterone. These hormones, in turn, increase production of other hormones and growth factors (50), which are vital for normal organ development. Drinking alcohol during this period of rapid growth and development (i.e., prior to or during puberty) may upset the critical hormonal balance necessary for normal development of organs, muscles, and bones. Studies in animals also show that consuming alcohol during puberty adversely affects the maturation of the reproductive system (51).

LT phys.— could affect organ development

LT phys.— possible disruption to reproductive system development

CONCLUSION

18 Today, alcohol is widely available and aggressively promoted throughout society. And alcohol use continues to be regarded, by many people, as a normal part of growing up. Yet underage drinking is dangerous, not only for the drinker but also for society, as evident by the number of alcohol-involved motor vehicle crashes, homicides, suicides, and other injuries.

19 People who begin drinking early in life run the risk of developing serious alcohol problems, including alcoholism, later in life. They also are at greater risk for a variety of adverse consequences, including risky sexual activity and poor performance in school.

20 Identifying adolescents at greatest risk can help stop problems before they develop. And innovative, comprehensive approaches to prevention are showing success in reducing experimentation with alcohol as well as the problems that accompany alcohol use by young people.

Full text of this publication is available on NIAAA's World Wide Web site at http://www.niaaa.nih.gov. All material contained in the Alcohol Alert is in the public domain and may be used or reproduced without permission from NIAAA. Citation of the source is appreciated. Copies of the Alcohol Alert are available free of charge from the National Institute on Alcohol Abuse and Alcoholism Publications Distribution Center, P.O. Box 10686, Rockville, MD 20849–0686.

© 2009. Teacher's Discovery®

Task 2.   Mark then created a chart that would help him organize the information he had collected. Under each of the topic headings, he listed the information from the article that belongs in each category. Since these are the headings that he will use for the note cards, they tell him what information to put on each card. In addition, because the chart lists the specific information he will use to support his thesis, he can see with a quick glance which subtopics he needs to find more information about. This chart will also help Mark organize his outline in the next step.

Short-term Effects (both mind and body)	Long-term Effects (physical)	Long-term Effects (psychological)
1. Injuries (falls/burns)	1. Death	1. Danger of alcoholism later in life
2. Drowsiness, lack of coordination, hangover	2. Liver damage	2. Encourages risky behaviors
	3. Could affect organ development	3. Possible impairment of long-term memory and learning skills
	4. Possible disruption to reproductive system development	

Note:

Highlighting or annotating in library books and magazines is not allowed, but making copies of pages with useful information to highlight later is allowed. Using printouts from electronic sources also makes these steps easier.

© 2009. Teacher's Discovery®

Practice using Mark's technique for finding relevant information. Follow the same procedure to identify the information in the article to best support the topics that Mark has identified as important for proving his thesis.

Practice Exercise for Finding Useful Information

Task 1. Photocopy the worksheets on page pages 146-149 of this book. It is the article "Getting Stupid" by Bernice Wuethrich, which appeared in *Discover*, March 2001, pages 56-63. The paragraphs have been numbered for easy reference.

With a highlighter, pen, or pencil, specify the sections of the article that Mark might use for his paper. Look for both **short-term** and **long-term effects**, and for effects on both **body** and **mind, as they pertain to teens**. Identify these highlighted sections with brief headings and notes. Use the same abbreviations as Mark: ST for short-term effects, LT for long-term effects, Phys. for physical effects, and Psych. for psychological effects.

Ignore other information and details not immediately relevant to these topics.

Task 2. Now read the second version of the same article located on pages 58-61 to see how Mark's notes turned out. The paragraphs that Mark selected as relevant are highlighted, and his notes are located in the margins.

Notice that, just as in the previous article, Mark has marked only those paragraphs that contain information about the **effects** of teenage drinking.

Task 3. Compare your "Getting Stupid" worksheet highlighting with Mark's, and see if it agrees. Bear in mind that annotating and highlighting are preliminary steps; what eventually ends up on the note cards may change depending on what further reading uncovers.

Task 4. Using the chart on the last page of the worksheets, list under the proper topic headings the information that belongs in each catagory.

Mark's Future Tasks

After copying down the relevant information from this article onto his note cards, Mark will go on to his next source, perhaps an article in *Alcoholism: Clinical and Experimental Research* or in the *American Journal of Psychiatry*.

With each new source, he will repeat the procedure, putting the information he finds on additional note cards with the same topic headings: Short-term Effects; Long-term Physical Effects; Long-term Psychological Effects. He will probably put subtopic headings on his note cards (for example, Memory Loss, Attention Deficit, and Personality Changes).

If he finds additional effects, he will create another subtopic heading and take down additional information on note cards under that heading. As he records information, he'll add his own comments or questions, keeping them distinct by using braces, ink or highlighting, or some other method to separate source material from his own observations.

© 2009. Teacher's Discovery®

Getting Stupid

New research indicates that teenagers who drink too much may lose as much as 10 percent of their brainpower— the difference between passing and failing in school … and in life

By Bernice Wuethrich

ST phys.— passing out, alcohol poisoning

ST phys.— vomiting, choking hazard

1   Sarah, a high school senior, drinks in moderation, but many of her friends do not. At one party, a classmate passed out after downing more than 20 shots of hard liquor and had to be rushed to a local emergency room. At another party a friend got sick, so Sarah made her drink water, dressed her in a sweatshirt to keep her warm, and lay her in bed, with a bucket on the floor. Then she brushed the girl's long hair away from her face so that it wouldn't get coated with vomit. "Every weekend, drinking is the only thing people do. Every single party has alcohol," says Sarah. (The names of the teenagers in these stories have been changed to protect their privacy.)

2   The most recent statistics from the U.S. Substance Abuse and Mental Health Services Administration's National Household Survey on Drug Abuse indicate that nearly 7 million youths between the ages of 12 and 20 binge-drink at least once a month. And despite the fact that many colleges have cracked down on drinking, Henry Wechsler of the Harvard School of Public Health says that two of every five college students still binge-drink regularly. For a male that means downing five or more drinks in a row; for a female it means consuming four drinks in one session at least once in a two-week period.

LT phys.— cirrhosis, heart disease

LT psych.— brain damage

3   Few teens seem to worry much about what such drinking does to their bodies. Cirrhosis of the liver is unlikely to catch up with them for decades, and heart disease must seem as remote as retirement. But new research suggests that young drinkers are courting danger. Because their brains are still developing well into their twenties, teens who drink excessively may be destroying significant amounts of mental capacity in ways that are more dramatic than in older drinkers.

ST phys.— motor skills

LT psych.— psychosis, memory loss

4   Scientists have long known that excessive alcohol consumption among adults over long periods of time can create brain damage, ranging from a mild loss of motor skills to psychosis and even the inability to form memories. But less has been known about the impact alcohol has on younger brains. Until recently, scientists assumed that a youthful brain is more resilient than an adult brain and could escape many of the worst ills of alcohol. But some researchers are now beginning to question this assumption. Preliminary results from several studies indicate that the younger the brain

is, the more it may be at risk. "The adolescent brain is a developing nervous system, and the things you do to it can change it," says Scott Swartzwelder, a neuropsychologist at Duke University and the U.S. Department of Veterans Affairs.

LT psych.— damage to hippocampus, prefrontal cortex; learning, memory, decision-making, reasoning

5   Teen drinkers appear to be most susceptible to damage in the hippocampus, a structure buried deep in the brain that is responsible for many types of learning and memory, and the prefrontal cortex, located behind the forehead, which is the brain's chief decision maker and voice of reason. Both areas, especially the prefrontal cortex, undergo dramatic change in the second decade of life.

6   Swartzwelder and his team have been studying how alcohol affects the hippocampus, an evolutionarily old part of the brain that is similar in rats and humans. Six years ago, when Swartzwelder published his first paper suggesting that alcohol disrupts the hippocampus more severely in adolescent rats than in adult rats, "people didn't believe it," he says. Since then, his research has shown that the adolescent brain is more easily damaged in the structures that regulate the acquisition and storage of memories.

LT psych.— memory

7   Learning depends on communication between nerve cells, or neurons, within the hippocampus. To communicate, a neuron fires an electrical signal down its axon, a single fiber extending away from the cell's center. In response, the axon releases chemical messengers, called neurotransmitters, which bind to receptors on the receiving branches of neighboring cells. Depending on the types of neurotransmitters released, the receiving cell may be jolted into action or settle more deeply into rest.

8   But the formation of memories requires more than the simple firing or inhibition of nerve cells. There must be some physical change in the hippocampal neurons that represents the encoding of new information. Scientists believe that this change occurs in the synapses, the tiny gaps between neurons that neurotransmitters traverse. Repeated use of synapses seems to increase their ability to fire up connecting cells. Laboratory experiments on brain tissue can induce this process, called long-term potentiation. Researchers assume that something similar takes place in the intact living brain, although it is impossible to observe directly. Essentially, if the repetitive neural reverberations

© 2009. Teacher's Discovery®

are strong enough, they burn in new patterns of synaptic circuitry to encode memory, just as the more often a child recites his ABCs, the better he knows them.

9 Swartzwelder's first clue that alcohol powerfully disrupts memory in the adolescent brain came from studying rat hippocampi. He found that alcohol blocks long-term potentiation in adolescent brain tissue much more than in adult tissue. Next, Swartzwelder identified a likely explanation. Long-term potentiation— and thus memory formation— relies in large part on the action of a neurotransmitter known as glutamate, the brain's chemical king-pin of neural excitation. Glutamate strengthens a cell's electrical stimulation when it binds to a docking port called the NMDA receptor. If the receptor is blocked, so is long-term potentiation, and thus memory formation. Swartzwelder found that exposure to the equivalent of just two beers inhibits the NMDA receptors in the hippocampal cells of adolescent rats, while more than twice as much is required to produce the same effect in adult rats. These findings led him to suspect that alcohol consumption might have a dramatic impact on the ability of adolescents to learn. So he set up a series of behavioral tests.

LT psych.— memory formation, ability to learn

10 First, Swartzwelder's team dosed adolescent and adult rats with alcohol and ran them through maze-learning tests. Compared with the adult rats, the adolescents failed miserably. To see whether similar results held true for humans, Swartzwelder recruited a group of volunteers aged 21 to 29 years old. He couldn't use younger subjects because of laws that forbid drinking before age 21. He chose to split the volunteers into two groups: 21 to 24 years old and 25 to 29 years old. "While I wouldn't argue that these younger folks are adolescents, even in their early twenties their brains are still developing," Swartzwelder says. After three drinks, with a blood-alcohol level slightly below the National Highway Traffic Safety Administration's recommended limit— .08 percent— the younger group's learning was impaired 25 percent more than the older group's.

LT psych.— learning impairment

11 Intrigued by these results, Swartzwelder's colleague Aaron White, a biological psychologist at Duke, set out to discover how vulnerable the adolescent brain is to long-term damage. He gave adolescent and adult rats large doses of alcohol every other day for 20 days— the equivalent of a 150-pound human chugging 24 drinks in a row. Twenty days after the last binge, when the adolescent rats had reached adulthood, White trained them in a maze-memory task roughly akin to that performed by a human when remembering the location of his car in a parking garage.

12 Both the younger and older rats performed equally well when sober. But when intoxicated, those who had binged as adolescents performed much worse. "Binge alcohol exposure in

adolescence appears to produce long-lasting changes in brain function," White says. He suspects that early damage caused by alcohol could surface whenever the brain is taxed. He also suspects that the NMDA receptor is involved, because just as alcohol in the system inhibits the receptor, the drug's withdrawal overstimulates it— which can kill the cell outright.

LT psych.— damage to memory functions

13 *During the fall semester last year, at least 11 college students died from alcohol-related causes— at California State University at Chico, Colgate University in New York, Old Dominion University in Virginia, the University of Michigan, Vincennes University in Kentucky, Washington and Lee University in Virginia, and Washington State University. No one knows how many other students were rushed to emergency rooms for alcohol poisoning, but at Duke, 11 students had visited local ERs in just the first three weeks of school, and in only one night of partying, three students from the University of Tennessee were hospitalized.*

ST phys.— alcohol poisoning

LT phys.—death

14 Students who drink heavily sometimes joke that they are killing a few brain cells. New research suggests that this is not funny. Some of the evidence is anatomical: Michael De Bellis at the University of Pittsburgh Medical Center used magnetic resonance imaging to compare the hippocampi of subjects 14 to 21 years old who abused alcohol to the hippocampi of those who did not. He found that the longer and the more a young person had been drinking, the smaller his hippocampus. The average size difference between healthy teens and alcohol abusers was roughly 10 percent. That is a lot of brain cells.

LT psych.— shrinking hippocampus, loss of brain cells

15 De Bellis speculates that the shrinkage may be due to cell damage and death that occurs during withdrawal from alcohol. Withdrawal is the brain's way of trying to get back to normal after prolonged or heavy drinking. It can leave the hands jittery, set off the classic headache, generate intense anxiety, and even provoke seizures, as neurons that had adjusted to the presence of alcohol try to adjust to its absence. Because alcohol slows down the transmission of nerve signals— in part by stopping glutamate from activating its NMDA receptors— nerve cells under the influence react by increasing the number and sensitivity of these receptors. When drinking stops, the brain is suddenly stuck with too many hyperactive receptors.

ST phys.— jitters, headache, anxiety, seizures

16 Mark Prendergast, a neuroscientist at the University of Kentucky, recently revealed one way these hyperactive receptors kill brain cells. First, he exposed rat hippocampal slices to alcohol for 10 days, then removed the alcohol. Following withdrawal, he stained the tissue with a fluorescent dye that lit up dead and dying cells. When exposed to an alcohol concentration of about .08 percent, cell death increased some 25 percent above the

LT psych.— brain cell death

© 2009. Teacher's Discovery®

baseline. When concentrations were two or three times higher, he wrote in a recent issue of *Alcoholism: Clinical and Experimental Research*, the number of dead cells shot up to 100 percent above the baseline.

17   Prendergast says that the younger brain tissue was far more sensitive. Preadolescent tissue suffered four to five times more cell death than did adult tissue. In all cases, most of the death occurred in hippocampal cells that were packed with NMDA receptors. To home in on the cause, he treated another batch of brain slices with the drug MK-801, which blocks NMDA receptors. He reasoned that if overexcitability during alcohol withdrawal was causing cell death, blocking the receptors should minimize the carnage. It did, by about 75 percent.

18   Now Prendergast is examining what makes the receptors so lethal. By tracking radioactive calcium, he found that the overexcited receptors open floodgates that allow calcium to swamp the cell. Too much calcium can turn on suicide genes that cause the neuron to break down its own membrane. Indeed, that is exactly what Prendergast observed during alcohol withdrawal: Overactive receptors opened wide, and the influx of calcium became a raging flood.

19   Prendergast says that four or five drinks may cause a mild withdrawal. And, according to Harvard's Wechsler, 44 percent of college students binge in this manner. More alarming, 23 percent of them consume 72 percent of all the alcohol that college students drink.

20   *Chuck was 15 the first time he binged— on warm beers chugged with friends late at night in a vacant house. Six years later, celebrating his 21st birthday, he rapidly downed four shots of vodka in his dorm room. Then he and his friends drove through the snowy night to a sorority party at a bar, where he consumed another 16 drinks. Chuck's friends later told him how the rest of the night unfolded. He danced in a cage. He spun on the floor. He careened around the parking lot with a friend on his back. Halfway home, he stumbled out of the car and threw up. A friend half carried him home down frozen roads at 2 a.m. "I don't remember any of this," Chuck says. But he does remember the hangover he lived with for two days, as his brain and body withdrew from the booze.*

> ST phys.—
> bizarre behavior, vomiting, memory loss, hangover

21   Recent human studies support a conclusion Prendergast drew from his molecular experiments: The greatest brain damage from alcohol occurs during withdrawal. At the University of California at San Diego and the VA San Diego Health Care System, Sandra Brown, Susan Tapert, and Gregory Brown have been following alcohol-dependent adolescents for eight years. Repeated testing shows that problem drinkers perform

> LT psych.—
> poor performance on tests of cognition, learning

more poorly on tests of cognition and learning than do nondrinkers. Furthermore, "the single best predictor of neuropsychological deficits for adolescents is withdrawal symptoms," says principal investigator Sandra Brown.

22   The psychologists recruited a group of 33 teenagers aged 15 and 16, all heavy drinkers. On average, each teen had used alcohol more than 750 times— the equivalent of drinking every day for two and a half years. Bingeing was common: The teens downed an average of eight drinks at each sitting. The researchers matched drinkers with nondrinkers of the same gender and similar age, IQ, socioeconomic background, and family history of alcohol use. Then, three weeks after the drinkers had their last drink, all the teens took a two-hour battery of tests.

23   The teens with alcohol problems had a harder time recalling information, both verbal and nonverbal, that they had learned 20 minutes earlier. Words such as apple and football escaped them. The performance difference was about 10 percent. "It's not serious brain damage, but it's the difference of a grade, a pass or a fail," Tapert says. Other tests evaluated skills needed for map learning, geometry, or science. Again, there was a 10 percent difference in performance.

> LT psych.—
> recall, skills for map reading, geometry, science

24   "The study shows that just several years of heavy alcohol use by youth can adversely affect their brain functions in ways that are critical to learning," Sandra Brown says. She is following the group of teenagers until they reach age 30, and some have already passed 21. "Those who continue to use alcohol heavily are developing attentional deficits in addition to the memory and problem-solving deficits that showed up early on," Brown says. "In the past we thought of alcohol as a more benign drug. It's not included in the war on drugs. This study clearly demonstrates that the most popular drug is also an incredibly dangerous drug."

> LT psych.—
> attention deficits; memory and problem-solving deficits

25   Brown's research team is also using functional magnetic resonance imaging to compare the brain function of alcohol abusers and nondrinkers. Initial results show that brains of young adults with a history of alcohol dependence are less active than the brains of nondrinkers during tasks that require spatial working memory (comparable to the maze task that White conducted on rats). In addition, the adolescent drinkers seem to exhibit greater levels of brain activity when they are exposed to alcohol-related stimuli. For instance, when the drinkers read words such as wasted or tequila on a screen, the nucleus accumbens— a small section of the brain associated with craving— lights up.

> LT psych.—
> reduced brain activity, increased craving after stimuli

26   The nucleus accumbens is integral to the brain's socalled pleasure circuit, which scientists now believe undergoes major remodeling during adolescence. Underlying the pleasure circuit is the neurotransmitter dopamine. Sex, food, and

© 2009. Teacher's Discovery®

many drugs, including alcohol, can all induce the release of dopamine, which creates feelings of pleasure and in turn encourages repetition of the original behavior. During adolescence, the balance of dopamine activity temporarily shifts away from the nucleus accumbens, the brain's key pleasure and reward center, to the prefrontal cortex. Linda Spear, a developmental psychobiologist at Binghamton University in New York, speculates that as a result of this shift in balance, teenagers may find drugs less rewarding than earlier or later in life. And if the drugs produce less of a kick, more will be needed for the same effect. "In the case of alcohol, this may lead to binge drinking," she says.

LT psych.— need for increased amounts of alcohol to cause pleasure

27   *When Lynn was a freshman in high school, she liked to hang out at her friend John's apartment. More often than not, his father would be drinking beer. "He was like, 'Help yourself,'" Lynn says. Friends would come over and play drinking games until four or five in the morning. The longer the games continued, the tougher the rules became, doubling and tripling the number of drinks consumed. One night, Lynn came home drunk. Her mother talked her through her options, sharing stories of relatives who had ruined their lives drinking. Lynn struggled with her choices. A year later she still drinks, but she's kept a pact with her girlfriends to stop bingeing.*

28   During adolescence, the prefrontal cortex changes more than any other part of the brain. At around age 11 or 12, its neurons branch out like crazy, only to be seriously pruned back in the years that follow. All this tumult is to good purpose. In the adult brain, the prefrontal cortex executes the thought processes adolescents struggle to master: the ability to plan ahead, think abstractly, and integrate information to make sound decisions.

LT psych.— damage to prefrontal cortex; planning, abstract thinking, integration of information

29   Now there is evidence that the prefrontal cortex and associated areas are among those most damaged in the brains of bingeing adolescents. Fulton Crews, director of the Center for Alcohol Studies at the University of North Carolina at Chapel Hill, has studied the patterns of cell death in the brains of adolescent and adult rats after four-day drinking bouts. While both groups showed damage in the back areas of the brain and in the frontally located olfactory bulb, used for smell, only the adolescents suffered brain damage in other frontal areas.

30   That youthful damage was severe. It extended from the rat's olfactory bulb to the interconnected parts of the brain that process sensory information and memories to make associations, such as "This smell and the sight of that wall tell me I'm in a place where I previously faced down an enemy." The regions of cell death in the rat experiment corresponded to the human prefrontal cortex and to parts of the limbic system.

LT psych.— ability to process sensory information and memories, make associations

The limbic system, which includes the 31 hippocampus, changes throughout adolescence, according to recent work by Jay Giedd at the National Institute of Mental Health in Bethesda, Maryland. The limbic system not only encodes memory but is also mobilized when a person is hungry or frightened or angry; it helps the brain process survival impulses. The limbic system and the prefrontal cortex must work in concert for a person to make sound decisions.

LT psych.— damage to limbic system: memory, survival impulses, ability to make sound decisions

Damage to the prefrontal cortex and the 32 limbic system is especially worrisome because they play an important role in the formation of an adult personality. "Binge drinking could be making permanent long-term changes in the final neural physiology, which is expressed as personality and behavior in the individual," Crews says. But he readily acknowledges that such conclusions are hypothetical. "It's very hard to prove this stuff. You can't do an experiment in which you change people's brains."

LT psych.— permanent damage to neural physiology; changes in personality, behavior

Nonetheless, evidence of the vulnerability 33 of young people to alcohol is mounting. A study by Bridget Grant of the National Institute on Alcohol Abuse and Alcoholism shows that the younger someone is when he begins to regularly drink alcohol, the more likely that individual will eventually become an alcoholic. Grant found that 40 percent of the drinkers who got started before age 15 were classified later in life as alcohol dependent, compared with only 10 percent of those who began drinking at age 21 or 22. Overall, beginning at age 15, the risk of future alcohol dependence decreased by 14 percent with each passing year of abstention.

LT psych.— danger of alcoholism

The study leaves unanswered whether early 34 regular drinking is merely a marker of later abuse or whether it results in long-term changes in the brain that increase the later propensity for abuse. "It's got to be both," Crews says. For one thing, he points out that studies of rats and people have shown that repeated alcohol use makes it harder for a person— or a rat— to learn new ways of doing things, rather than repeating the same actions over and over again. In short, the way alcohol changes the brain makes it increasingly difficult over time to stop reaching for beer after beer after beer.

LT psych.— difficulty learning new ways of doing things

Ultimately, the collateral damage caused 35 by having so many American adolescents reach for one drink after another may be incalculable. "People in their late teens have been drinking heavily for generations. We're not a society of idiots, but we're not a society of Einsteins either," says Swartzwelder. "What if you've compromised your function by 7 percent or 10 percent and never known the difference?"

Bernice Wuethrich/©2001.
Reprinted with permission of Discover Magazine.

© 2009. Teacher's Discovery®

Using Relevant Material

This section provides some examples of how to pick out the appropriate information from the books, magazines, websites, and other sources. Sharpen this skill before actually beginning to fill out the note cards.

How to Identify Relevant Material

Task 1.   To find relevant passages, learn to skim (to read rapidly through) looking for facts, ideas, quotations, statistics, or examples to support major supporting topics. Although sometimes it is necessary to study a passage carefully, it is not always needed when looking for useful information. Where possible, use the table of contents and index to help locate key passages.

Task 2.   With thesis statement and topic headings in mind, zero in on passages that can be used. Take down key information word for word, ignoring the rest. Copy only what is relevant.

Example 1

Here is how Dan managed this step. He was doing research on the jazz singer Billie Holiday for an oral presentation in which he planned to tell something about her life and career, and to play some tapes of her singing. His topic headings were **Early Life**, **Career**, and **Personality**. He looked at her autobiography, where she devotes several chapters to her childhood. Dan was looking for an incident that would be typical of the hardships she endured. Of the many possibilities, he finally chose one. The note card he prepared looked like this.

> *Childhood and Early Life*   *Holiday 6-7*
>
> *All of us were crowded in that little house like fishes. I had to sleep in the same bed with Henry and Elsie, and Henry used to wet it every night. It made (7) me mad and sometimes I'd get up and sit in a chair until morning. Then my cousin Ida would come in the morning, see the bed, accuse me of wetting it, and start beating me. When she was upset she'd beat me something awful. Not with a strap, not with a spank on the ass, but with her fist or a whip.*

When Dan wrote his rough draft, he used the information on the card in the paragraph below. Notice that he has thoroughly paraphrased the material, using only a brief direct quotation, and he has documented it accurately. He has also added his own observation to the paragraph by speculating about the effect of this early violence on Holiday's personality.[9]

> After her father went on the road with the musical group, McKinney's Cotton Pickers, Holiday's mother sent her to live with her grandparents and a number of other relatives. The house was small, and living conditions were difficult. Holiday had to share a bed with her Aunt Ida's two small children, one of whom usually wet the bed. Her aunt blamed Holiday, even though she was not guilty, and her aunt frequently beat her "with her fists or a whip" (Holiday 6-7). The abuse she suffered as a child undoubtedly left a mark on Holiday, who never stopped hating Aunt Ida. She was later prone to use violence herself, probably a consequence of experiencing violence as a child. But she also learned to be a survivor, a skill she needed throughout her trouble-filled life.

© 2009. Teacher's Discovery®

Summarizing- just main ideas
Paraphrasing- put idea in own words, one idea

─**Example 2**──────────────────────────

Sarah is writing about the importance of symbolism in *Adventures of Huckleberry Finn*. Under the topic heading The River, she recorded on Card 1 the following passage from T. S. Eliot's introduction to that novel:

The River   Eliot 325

It is the River that controls the voyage of Huck and Jim; that will not let them land at Cairo, where Jim could have reached freedom; it is the River that separates them and deposits Huck for a time in the Grangerford household; the River re-unites them, and then compels upon them the unwelcome company of the King and the Duke. Recurrently we are reminded of its presence and its power.

Card 1

Later, Sarah found some relevant information in Leo Marx's essay "Mr. Eliot, Mr. Trilling, and Huckleberry Finn." Her word-for-word notes, under the same topic heading The River but on Card 2, look like this:

The River   Marx 334

Then there is the river; after each adventure Huck and Jim return to the raft and the river. Both Mr. Trilling and Mr. Eliot speak eloquently of the river as a source of unity, and they refer to the river as a god. ... It is a source of food and beauty and terror and serenity of mind. But above all, it provides motion; it is the means by which Huck and Jim move away from a menacing civilization.

Card 2

In her rough draft, Sarah wrote the following paragraph to introduce her discussion of the various levels of symbolic meaning that critics have attributed to the river. Notice that she has thoroughly paraphrased the borrowed material, and she has documented it correctly.[10]

> Many critics have recognized the river as a major symbol in *Huckleberry Finn*, and they have suggested many different interpretations. But whatever its symbolic value, the river plays a crucial role in the narrative. It determines the action, taking Huck and Jim past Cairo and preventing Jim's escape up the Ohio River. The Mississippi River separates them, and it brings them together again. It brings them adventures, both joyful and terrifying (Eliot 325). Although some incidents take place away from the river, the most important action—especially Huck's decisions and discoveries—all occurs on the raft. The river sustains them on their journey, providing fish and occasional salvage. It brings them, briefly at least, a peaceful, idyllic existence, and its current carries them "away from a menacing civilization" (Marx 334). Ironically, it takes them farther into the Deep South, where Jim's quest for freedom will be even more difficult.

──

[9] The Billie Holiday example is based on Holiday, Billie. *Lady Sings the Blues*. New York: Avon, 1976. Print.
[10] Articles cited are in Clemens, Samuel L., "Adventures of Huckleberry Finn." *Norton Critical Editions*, New York: Norton, 1962. xx-xx. Print.

© 2009. Teacher's Discovery®

Composing Note Cards

Researchers take notes in a variety of different ways. Traditionally, students laboriously hand-copied data onto individual note cards labeled by topic headings. Nowadays students frequently cut the data from copies of their sources and glue or tape them to note cards. Some prefer to use a computer to cut-and-paste electronic data to word files organized by topic. Others swear by one of the many word processing programs that recreate cards digitally and can be linked to source cards. All of the methods, no matter which is employed, share some similarities:

- Selected information is recorded.
- Original sources of information are identified.
- Information can be organized topically.

Additionally, all effective methods

- provide convenient ways to organize and retrieve information.
- require selectivity in note taking.
- help prevent inadvertent plagiarism.
- provide quick means of checking information accuracy in the final product.

Although any method that accomplishes these tasks can be effective, teachers may prefer or require use of a specific method. Generally, many writers and most teachers still prefer a more traditional note card method that relies on the use of physical cards for recording the information found, hereafter referred to as **borrowed material**.

Although using a photocopying machine or the cut-and-paste function on a computer can be helpful, it doesn't do the job of **selecting relevant material and placing it under the right heading**, so it can't replace either a researcher's judgment or the organizational benefits of note cards. Nor can simply printing out articles and annotating or highlighting them replace the note card method, as this does not allow for efficiently grouping information by topic. If the teacher subscribes to a specific method of note taking other than the one described here, that teacher will, most likely, provide special instructions.

Refer to this sample note card while reading through the tasks of the note-taking process.

Example: Note Card

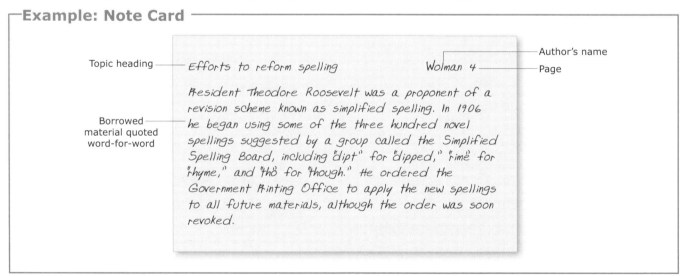

Topic heading — Efforts to reform spelling   Wolman 4 — Author's name / Page

Borrowed material quoted word-for-word —

President Theodore Roosevelt was a proponent of a revision scheme known as simplified spelling. In 1906 he began using some of the three hundred novel spellings suggested by a group called the Simplified Spelling Board, including "dipt" for "dipped," "rime" for "rhyme," and "tho" for "though." He ordered the Government Printing Office to apply the new spellings to all future materials, although the order was soon revoked.

© 2009. Teacher's Discovery®

Tasks in Note Taking

Task 1. **Note cards.** Use 4 x 6-inch or 5 x 8-inch index cards, NOT 3 x 5-inch, which are too small. It takes approximately 20 to 25 index cards for a five-page paper.

On an additional card, write the revised thesis statement and list the three or more major supporting topics. Keep these constantly in mind while taking notes so time is not wasted copying useless material.

Use a pen and write legibly.

Task 2. **Topic headings.** Label each card with a topic heading that identifies the subject matter on the card. Remember that these topics correspond to the major supporting topics in the working outline. Here are some typical topic headings:

> **Example**
>
> *Problem-Solving Ability* (for a paper on dolphin intelligence)
>
> *Damage to Hemlock Forests* (for a paper on the effects of acid rain)
>
> *Color Symbolism* (for a paper on symbolism in James Joyce's *Portrait of the Artist as a Young Man*)

Have no more than three or four major supporting topic headings. If there appear to be more supporting topics, consider reorganizing them as **subheadings** under the **major topic headings**. For example, under the major supporting topic heading *Problem-Solving Ability*, consider using the subheadings *Locating Hidden Objects, Negotiating a Maze,* and *Avoiding Danger.*

Under the major supporting topic heading *Color Symbolism*, subcategorize as *Red, Green,* and *Black.* Under *Damage to Hemlock Forests*, the note cards might include subheadings that list specific kinds of damage.

Hint:

It might be useful to head a few cards *Miscellaneous*, or *General Information*, for items that do not fit into specific categories but might prove useful somewhere.

© 2009. Teacher's Discovery®

Task 3. **Formatting.** In the upper right corner of each card, write the author's last name and the page number on which the information is located. If there is no author, as in an unsigned editorial or newspaper article, use the first important word of the title. If there is no page number, as with many Internet sources, use the paragraph number (if provided). If there are no page or paragraph numbers, omit it. The name or first important word of the title links the note card to the source card, the place where the complete publication information is recorded.

> ## Note:
>
> Do not forget to include page numbers on note cards when it is available. MLA style requires the inclusion of page numbers in all of the paper's parenthetical citations, and APA style requires the inclusion of page numbers with a direct quotation. Therefore, record the page numbers as relevant information is found to prevent the need to return to each original source as the paper is composed.

Example

On a **source card** (3 x 5-inches), write:

Wolman, David. *Righting the Mother Tongue: From Olde English to Email, the Tangled Story of English Spelling.* New York: Collins, 2008. Print.

On the **note card** (4 x 6-inches), write only Wolman 4 in the upper right corner—the author's last name (Wolman) and the page number of the useful information (4). Now write the information found on page 4 planned for use in the paper, copying it accurately onto the card.

If there is a second Wolman source card, say for Wolman's article "To Bee or Not to Bee," then add "To Bee" between the author's name and page number (Wolman, "To Bee" 3) to those note cards to identify their source as the article. Add *Righting* (Wolman, *Righting* 4) to this note card and other note cards with information from the book.

Wolman, David. *Righting the Mother Tongue: From Olde English to Email, the Tangled Story of English Spelling.* New York: Collins, 2008. Print.

Efforts to reform spelling   Wolman 4

President Theodore Roosevelt was a proponent of a revision scheme known as simplified spelling. In 1906 he began using some of the three hundred novel spellings suggested by a group called the Simplified Spelling Board, including "dipt" for "dipped," "rime" for "rhyme," and "tho" for "though." He ordered the Government Printing Office to apply the new spellings to all future materials, although the order was soon revoked.

Topic Heading   Wolman, "To Bee" 4

Efforts to reform spelling   Wolman, *Righting* 4

President Theodore Roosevelt was a proponent of a revision scheme known as simplified spelling. In 1906 he began using some of the three hundred novel spellings suggested by a group called the Simplified Spelling Board, including "dipt" for "dipped," "rime" for "rhyme," and "tho" for "though." He ordered the Government Printing Office to apply the new spellings to all future materials, although the order was soon revoked.

Task 4.   **One idea per card.** Put only one idea or entry from one source on each card. This may include several sentences, but they should be continuous and should relate to the same subject.

> **Example**
>
> The information put on a particular card might be
>
> - the writer's description of a childhood incident.
> - a critic's interpretation of a symbol in a poem.
> - a stage in a natural process.
> - a historian's account of the reasons for Tecumseh's defeat at Maguaga.

Write on both sides of each card, and continue onto another card if necessary. Repeat author and page information on the second card (e.g., Wolman 4). If quoted material occurs on consecutive pages, insert the new page number on the card, as in the model on page 69.

Task 5.   **Record precisely.** Do not paraphrase or summarize the information; record it verbatim—word for word.

Omit what is not immediately pertinent to the topic. Use care in choosing material to quote; do not just copy everything in sight. Use an ellipsis (three spaced dots) to show omissions. If the author being quoted uses an ellipsis, then add ellipses and place them inside square brackets to distinguish which omission is not part of the original text. Use square brackets also to insert words needed for clarity: "[Marquez's] luminous narrative … rivals the most remarkable stories of man's struggles against the sea."

Do not enclose the card entry in quotation marks because **everything** listed is already established as a word-for-word copy of the original. **Paraphrasing** and **summarizing** will be used in the paper, but note cards should contain only material that is identical to the original source, and which may then be used for **direct quotation**. Accuracy includes capitalization, spelling, and punctuation.

Note:

Task 5 is critical in preventing plagiarism.

More suggestions:

- Consider marking information that may be especially important with an asterisk or highlighter.

- Add personal observations, comments and questions right on the note card, placing them inside braces to show that they are uniquely the researcher/writer's own observation and not borrowed material. These valuable personal notations will come in handy when the note cards are reviewed.

- Use different colored ink or highlighting to distinguish personal comments from the borrowed materials.

© 2009. Teacher's Discovery®

Task 6. **Relevance.** Ensure that the information on each card is relevant and confirm that the data conforms to the topic heading.

> ┌─**Example** ───
>
> A baseball player's lifetime batting average does not belong on a note card headed
>
> *Childhood.*
>
> A comment on Dickens's writing style should not be on a card with the heading
>
> *Characterization.*
>
> Information about the koala's mating behavior does not belong on a card headed
>
> *Food Supply.*

Task 7. **Follow through.** Prepare the cards for submission. When handing in note cards for a teacher's review, unless otherwise instructed, add a card on top listing student's name, teacher's name, and class. Include on this card the thesis statement as it currently is worded and the major supporting topics. Put a rubber band around the entire stack. Keep the note cards in a safe place. It may be a good idea to photocopy and then scan the note cards into a computer file, so that if the note cards are lost the information can be retrieved. When using a computer program to take and keep notes, save the digital file in at least two separate places.

Examples: Sample Note Cards

Card A is a note card that Todd prepared during his research on symbolism in *The Great Gatsby*. He headed a second stack of cards *The Green Light*. A third pile had the topic heading *Dr. Eckleberg's Eyes*. On each set of cards he took down only information pertinent to that particular topic—in this case, the importance of different symbols in Fitzgerald's novel.

Topic heading —

Wasteland Symbolism   Dyson 113

The action takes place in the "waste land" (this phrase is actually used), and is at one level, the study of a broken society. The "valley of ashes" in which Myrtle and Wilson live symbolizes the human situation in an age of chaos. It is "a certain desolate area of land" in which "ash-gray men" swarm dimly. ...This devitalized limbo is presided over by the eyes of Dr. T. J. Eckleberg.

Card A

Card B is from Melissa's paper on the role of race in modern American political elections. She recorded information from Barack Obama's book *The Audacity of Hope* on several cards, and then consulted other books and articles on minority candidates in recent political races to learn about the experiences of African American, Hispanic, and Asian candidates. Since her source cards include two different books by Obama—*The Audacity of Hope* and *Dreams From my Father*—she identified each one on her note cards with the author's last name and the first important word of the title.

Topic heading —

Obama funding   Obama, Audacity 240

Of the first $500,000 that I raised during the [Illinois Senate] primary, close to half came from black businesses and professionals. It was a black-owned radio station, WVON, that first began to mention my campaign on the Chicago airwaves, and a black-owned weekly newsmagazine, N-Digo, that first featured me on its cover. One of the first times I needed a corporate jet for the campaign, it was a black friend who lent me his.

Card B

Card C is part of Corey's research on the effects of insecticides. After looking at studies of DDT and other toxic substances, she split the topic into subtopics. Under the heading *long-term effects*, she recorded information about the insects' growing resistance to sprays, the increased mortality of birds that ate the insects, and the increased sterility of the birds that survived. Under *short-term effects*, she noted the immediate decrease of insects, reduction of typhus deaths, decrease in the spread of malaria, and the like.

Topic heading —
Sub heading —

Long-term Effects   Carson 267-8
Resistance to insecticides

Probably the first medical use of modern insecticides occurred in Italy when the Allied Military Command launched a successful attack on typhus by dusting enormous numbers of people with DDT. This was followed two years later by ... residual sprays for the control of malaria (268) mosquitoes. Only a year later the first signs of trouble appeared. Both houseflies and mosquitoes of the genus Culex began to show resistance to sprays.

Card C

© 2009. Teacher's Discovery®

Step 6 Summary

To locate relevant and useful information before taking notes:

- Identify at least three major topics to support the thesis statement.

- Photocopy the pages of library books or magazines, or print the article from an Internet source.

- Highlight text that supports the major topics, and make notations in the margins to link the information found to the topic headings and subheadings.

- Skim documents for relevant passages.

To prepare note cards:

- Take notes on 4 x 6-inch cards.

- Head each card with a Topic Heading; use subtopics if needed. Take down only information relevant to this topic.

- Put the author's name and the page number in the upper right corner.

- Copy word for word onto note cards the information that supports the thesis statement and major topics.

- Put only one entry or idea from a given source on each card.

- Record personal comments and ideas on note cards as well, making sure to keep these personal observations and questions separate and distinct from the borrowed material on the cards.

Step 7

Preparing to Write the Paper

Extending the Outline

Paraphrasing and Summarizing

Using Direct Quotation

Parenthetical Documentation

© 2009. Teacher's Discovery®

Extending the Outline

The preliminary outline constructed during Step 5 guided the note-taking procedure and helped organize the shape of the paper. Before writing, however, update this outline with the information recorded on the note cards. The extended outline should show the entire structure of the paper, including the order in which the borrowed information is presented. A good outline will keep the writer on track during the drafting process, preventing drifting toward unnecessary topics or diversions. Because the outline requires the student to clarify and organize the argument and the support presented in the paper, it is imperative that the outline be completed before any actual writing occurs. Students are sometimes tempted to skip the outline, thinking that their ideas will come together once they start writing; however, the outline actually makes the writing faster and easier.

Procedure for Extending the Outline

Task 1. Extend the topic outline by adding additional material from the research to the rough, tentative topic outline. A model of this outline is included in Appendix A. It is necessary to have a clear **topic sentence** to introduce each of the body sections of a paper.

> ### Note:
>
> We'll use the term **body sections** instead of **body paragraphs** since normally several paragraphs are needed to develop supporting ideas. Some books and some teachers call these **developmental paragraphs** and **developmental sections**.

Task 2. Compose a **topic sentence** to introduce each of the body sections of a paper.

A good topic sentence provides an overview of the major supporting topic that is being presented in this section of the paper, and it connects the major supporting topic to the thesis by explaining how it contributes to the overall argument of the paper.

Task 3. Write the latest version of the **thesis statement** at the top of the paper.

Do not try to write an opening paragraph or paragraphs now; leave it for later. The introduction, like the abstract in the scientific research report, provides an overview of the paper. Therefore, writing it last means that the overview will be as close as possible to the actual content presented in the paper.

© 2009. Teacher's Discovery®

Paraphrasing and Summarizing

One of the more difficult tasks students encounter when they compose a rough draft is successfully incorporating borrowed material into their papers. Step 7 reviews the necessary skills of paraphrasing, summarizing, and using direct quotations. It also provides instruction on the correct format for parenthetical citations.

Paraphrasing Rules

Most of the borrowed material used in a paper should be paraphrased. This means the student rewrites or restates the person's original ideas **in his/her own words**. Keep in mind the following rules:

Rule 1. **Understand.** Have a thorough understanding of the passage before paraphrasing it. Note key words and phrases, looking up definitions for any unfamiliar terms.

Rule 2. **Clarify and simplify.** Clarify and simplify in the paraphrase.

Rule 3. **Retain the meaning.** Retain the exact meaning of the original.

Rule 4. **Maintain the form.** Maintain approximately the same length, order of ideas, tone, and message. Do not use the same words and phrases except for the few that cannot be changed because they have no adequate synonyms or because a specific word is essential to the meaning of the passage.

Rule 5. **Personalize the style.** Develop and maintain a personal writing style throughout the paper, even when restating others' ideas, attitudes, and beliefs.

Rule 6. **Provide citations.** Provide in-text citations for all paraphrased material.

Read the following paragraph from page 140 of Charles C. Mann's book *1491: New Revelations of the Americas Before Columbus,* in which he describes the reaction of Cortez and his soldiers to their first sight of the capital city of the Aztec Empire, Tenochtitlan. Then examine both of the proposed paraphrases and decide which one is acceptable and why.

Example

Original:

> Tenochtitlan dazzled its invaders—it was bigger than Paris, Europe's greatest metropolis. The Spaniards gawped like yokels at the wide streets, ornately carved buildings, and markets bright with goods from hundreds of miles away. Boats flitted like butterflies around the three grand causeways that linked Tenochtitlan to the mainland. Long aqueducts conveyed water from the distant mountains across the lake and into the city. Even more astounding than the great temples and immense banners and colorful promenades were the botanical gardens—none existed in Europe. The same novelty attended the force of a thousand men that kept the crowded streets immaculate. (Streets that weren't ankle-deep in sewage! The conquistadors had never conceived of such a thing.)

Brandon's version:

The Conquistadors were astonished by what they saw in Tenochtitlan. The city was bigger than Paris, and it boasted wide streets, busy markets, and beautiful buildings. Huge causeways had been built for easy access to the mainland, and aqueducts brought fresh water into the city. In addition to these marvels, Cortez and his soldiers discovered things that were unheard of in Europe, including botanical gardens and sanitary living conditions maintained by public workers (Mann 140).

Alex's version:

Cortez and his men were amazed by Tenochtitlan. It was bigger than Paris, Europe's largest metropolis. The Spaniards were awed by its wide streets, ornately carved buildings, and markets with goods from hundreds of miles away. Three causeways connected the city to the mainland, and long aqueducts brought water from faraway mountains. The Conquistadtors were also astounded by the botanical gardens, which did not exist in Europe, as well as the group of 1,000 men who kept the streets clean (Mann 140).

When comparing Alex's and Brandon's paraphrasing, notice that Alex repeated many of the words of the original, using synonyms or slightly different forms: connected/linked, brought/conveyed, astounded/astounding. Alex's paraphrase also repeats exact phrases like "wide streets, ornately carved buildings, and markets" and "It was bigger than Paris, Europe's largest metropolis."

Practice

After reviewing the rules, try paraphrasing the following paragraph about the Botocudo, a group of South American Indians, from page 152 of the same book.

Original:

The Botocudo were an indigenous group that lived a few hundred miles north of what is now Rio de Janeiro. (The name comes from *botoque*, the derogatory Portuguese term for the big wooden discs that the Botocudo inserted in their lower lips and earlobes, distending them outward.) Although apparently never numerous, they resisted conquest so successfully that in 1801 the Portuguese colonial government formally launched a "just war against the cannibalistic Botocudo." There followed a century of intermittent strife, which slowly drove the Botocudo to extinction.

© 2009. Teacher's Discovery®

Summarizing Rules

A summary is a shortened version of a paraphrase. It retains the original writer's main idea and point of view but condenses the material. Like the paraphrase, it uses the writer's own words. Here are the rules:

Rule 1. Read the passage, paying attention to keywords, looking up definitions for any unfamiliar terms.

Rule 2. Restate the main facts and ideas, keeping the order.

Rule 3. Include essential information, but omit descriptive details, examples, illustrations, analogies, and anecdotes.

Rule 4. Try to shrink the passage to about one-third the length of the original.

Rule 5. Provide a parenthetical citation for the material being summarized.

Read the following excerpt from pages 7-8 in the introduction to *The Canon: A Whirligig Tour of the Beautiful Basics of Science* by Natalie Angier, and then compare the two summaries that follow. Do they convey the main idea of the original? Are any crucial points omitted? Has anything been added that was not in the original passage?

Example

Original:

> The arguments for greater scientific awareness and a more comfortable relationship with scientific reasoning are legion, and many have been flogged so often they're beginning to wheeze. A favorite thesis has it that people should know more about science because many of the vital issues of the day have a scientific component: think global warming, alternative energy, embryonic stem cell research, missile defense … [while] others propose that a scientifically astute public would be relatively shielded against superstitious, wishful thinking, flimflammery, and fraud. They would realize that the premise behind astrology was ludicrous, and that the doctor or midwife or taxi driver who helped deliver you exerted a far greater pull on you at your moment of birth than did the sun, moon, or any of the planets. They would accept that the fortune in their cookie at the Chinese restaurant was written either by a computer or a new hire at the Wonton Food factory in Queens. They would calculate their odds of winning the lottery, see how ridiculously tiny they were, and decide to stop buying lottery tickets, at which point the education budgets of at least thirty of our fifty states would collapse.

© 2009. Teacher's Discovery®

Sarah's version:

Angier cites two common arguments for increased awareness and understanding of science among the general public. The first is that some important current issues, such as global warming and stem cell research, require scientific knowledge in order to be responsibly understood. The second is that a stronger scientific inclination would encourage rational thinking among citizens and prevent them from silly choices and foolish superstitions (7-8).

Madison's version:

Angier believes that citizens should have greater scientific awareness and a more comfortable relationship with scientific reasoning because many of the most important social and political issues include scientific ideas and research, including global warming, alternative energy, embryonic stem cell research, and missile defense. In addition, she argues that a scientifically-minded public would better resist superstitions, like astrology and Chinese fortune cookie messages, as well as wishful thinking, like the sort that encourages people to waste their money on lottery tickets (7-8).

Note the differences between Sarah's and Madison's summaries and decide which one is better and why.

Practice

Summarize the paragraph below. It is from page 35 of the same book. Here the author discusses some common misperceptions that people have of science.[11]

Original:

People have the mistaken impression that the great revolutions in the history of science overturned prevailing wisdom. In fact, most of the great ideas subsumed their predecessors, gulped them whole and got bigger in the act. Albert Einstein did not prove that Isaac Newton was wrong. Instead, he showed that Newton's theories of motion and gravity were incomplete, and that new equations were needed to explain the behavior of objects under extreme circumstances, such as when tiny particles travel at or near the speed of light. Einstein made the pi wide and lighter and more exotically scalloped in space and time. But for the workaday trajectories of Earth spinning around the sun, or a baseball barreling toward a bat, or a brand-new earring sliding down a drain, Newton's laws of motion still apply.

---

[11] The cited material is from:
Angier, Natalie. *The Canon: A Whirligig Tour of the Beautiful Basics of Science. Boston:* Houghton, 2007. Print.
Mann, Charles C. *1491: New Revelations of the Americas Before Columbus.* New York: Vintage, 2006. Print.

© 2009. Teacher's Discovery®

Using Direct Quotation

Use direct quotation where the author's exact wording is essential to convey his or her meaning, tone, or language use. Primary and secondary sources, mentioned below, are explained in Step 1. Review the general rules first, and then look at the suggestions and examples for providing lead-ins and follow-ups for direct quotations. Because the process is complex, this chapter provides a number of examples from both student and professional writers.

General Rules of Using Direct Quotations

Rule 1. Use direct quotation of secondary source material

- to show excellence of ideas and expression.
- to explain complex material.
- to provide a way of introducing personal observations.

Rule 2. Use direct quotation of primary source material

- to provide evidence for judgments about a poem, speech, novel, case study, historical analysis, and the like.
- to provide specific examples to support interpretation of symbolism, analysis of character, suggestion of theme, and the like.

Rule 3. Copy the author's exact words and enclose them in quotation marks, following the rules for punctuation and capitalization:

- Place commas and periods inside quotation marks.
- Place colons, semi-colons, and dashes outside quotation marks.
- Place question marks or exclamation points inside quotation marks when they punctuate the quotation; place them outside when they punctuate the sentence.
- Use single quotation marks for a quotation within a quotation.

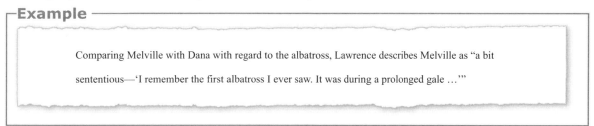

┌─ **Example** ─────────────────────────────────

Comparing Melville with Dana with regard to the albatross, Lawrence describes Melville as "a bit

sententious—'I remember the first albatross I ever saw. It was during a prolonged gale …'"

Here the writer quotes Lawrence, who quotes Melville, to illustrate the point about sententiousness.

- Alter initial capitals when a quotation forms a grammatical part of the sentence:

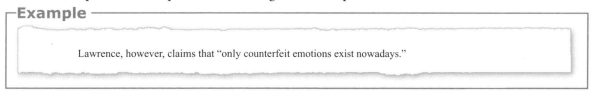

┌─ **Example** ─────────────────────────────────

Lawrence, however, claims that "only counterfeit emotions exist nowadays."

© 2009. Teacher's Discovery®

Otherwise, retain the capitalization in the quoted sentence:

Example

> Elsewhere Lawrence declares, "That was the pin he tortured himself on, like a pinned-down butterfly."

Rule 4. For every direct quotation, provide
- a lead-in—that is, introductory words or phrases.
- a follow-up—that is, an explanation of its meaning, relevance, or significance.
- a parenthetical citation—for example, "… to sleep forever" (Mudge 98).

Rule 5. Avoid monotony and maintain fluency by using a variety of methods to introduce direct quotations.

Example

A sharply contrasting attitude is that of Rush Limbaugh:

The distinguished literary critic Helen Vendler maintains …

According to 2008 Nobel Laureate Paul Krugman …

Noted economist Kenneth Galbraith presents a different point of view:

In support of this position, Senator John McCain (R-AZ) argues …

Rule 6. Use ellipses, that is, three dots, for omissions. Ellipses should be treated as a word for the purposes of punctuation and spacing. If the author being quoted has used ellipses points and it is necessary to omit a portion of the quote, use ellipses in square brackets […] to distinguish the edit from the author's edit.

Example

Original Passage:

> It was thus that He recovered from being a God. … He had made everything too beautiful. … The devil is simply God's moment of idleness at the end of that seventh day.

Direct quotation:

> Explaining the serpent at the tree of knowledge, Friedrich Nietzsche writes: "It was thus that He recovered from being a God. … […] The devil is simply God's moment of idleness at the end of that seventh day" (909).

© 2009. Teacher's Discovery®

Rule 7. Use [*sic*] to indicate the retention of archaic or unusual spelling within an original quote. For example, if quoting the sentence "The lost aviators poured [*sic*] over their maps," the bracketed word *sic* acknowledges that the source's use of *poured* is inaccurate; the proper usage should be *pored*. When a minor change is needed in the wording of a direct quotation, for example, to change a pronoun or a verb tense, insert that needed word in brackets.

Example

Original Passage:

> And it must be understood that a prince, and especially a new prince, cannot observe all those things which are considered good in men, being often obliged, in order to maintain the state, to act against faith, against charity, against humanity, and against religion.

Direct quotation:

> In explaining how the ruler must keep faith with his subjects, Machiavelli argues that "a prince, and especially a new prince, … [is] often obliged … to act against faith, against charity, against humanity, and against religion" (102-103).

Rule 8. For quotations longer than four lines (40 or more words for APA), start a new line (enter), indent the entire quotation one inch from the left margin, double space, omit quotation marks, and place the citation outside the closing punctuation.

Example of a blocked quote

> Kafka's yearning for a future with his lover, Milena, is tempered by his realization that this future is impossible. In a letter to her, he writes:
>
> > Why, Milena, do you write about our common future which will never be, or is that why you write about it? Even when we were discussing it in Vienna one evening, I had the feeling we were looking for somebody we knew very well and missed very much and whom we consequently kept calling with the most beautiful names, but there was no answer; how could he answer, since he wasn't there, nor anywhere nearby. (204)

Rule 9. Remember that a research paper should be a personal presentation of thoroughly assimilated material in which direct quotations are used sparingly. Directly quoted material should constitute no more than ten percent of the final paper.

© 2009. Teacher's Discovery®

Lead-ins for Quotations in a Literary Analysis Essay

Choose between paraphrasing and direct quotation

┌Example

In an essay on Holden's development over the course of the novel, *The Catcher in the Rye,* Jessica writes the following topic sentence: Holden reveals his inability to accept responsibility and to behave in a mature way by refusing to take school seriously.

She could support this using paraphrase:

> Holden explains that his present school, Pencey Prep, has just kicked him out for academic reasons (4).

> He dropped out of two other schools, the Whooton School and Elkton Hills (13).

Or she could use direct quotation:

> Holden explains that he isn't returning to Pencey Prep: "They kicked me out. I wasn't supposed to come back after Christmas vacation, on account of I was flunking four subjects and not applying myself and all. They gave me frequent warnings …" (4).

> The reader learns about Holden's previous academic failures through his conversation with Mr. Spencer, who remarks, "If I'm not mistaken, I believe you had some difficulty at the Whooton School and at Elkton Hills" (13).

> Holden explains why: "One of the biggest reasons I left Elkton Hills was because I was surrounded by phonies. … They were coming in the goddam window. For instance, they had this headmaster, Mr. Haas, that was the phoniest bastard I ever met in my life" (13-14).

© 2009. Teacher's Discovery®

Rules for Leading into Direct Quotations in Literary Analysis

Rule 1. Never insert a direct quotation without a lead-in, that is, an introductory phrase indicating the speaker or explaining the context.

Rule 2. If a complete sentence is used to introduce a quotation that is itself a complete sentence, use a colon before the quotation.

Rule 3. A comma is often appropriate after the lead-in when it indicates the speaker: Stephen Pinker observes, "Philosophy today gets no respect"; or Jared Diamond laments, "Alas, some clever microbes don't just cave in to our immune defenses."

Rule 4. Often it is best to use only part of a direct quotation and to paraphrase the rest.

Example

> Holden explains that he was "surrounded by phonies," and that he disliked the headmaster (13).

Rule 5. Use direct quotations sparingly. Use longer quotations only when they are essential in a discussion of diction, imagery, syntax, or other elements in order to discuss them clearly.

Example

If Jessica is discussing Holden's moment of illumination at the carousel, when he realizes that adults must let children grow up, she might need to quote the entire passage if that is a major point in her essay. She might write:

> Almost at the end of the story, Holden has a moment of illumination when he realizes that adults must let children grow up. He observes:
>
> > All the kids kept trying to grab the gold ring, and so was old Phoebe, and I was sort of afraid she'd fall off the goddam horse, but I didn't say anything or do anything. The thing with kids is, if they want to grab for the gold ring, you have to let them do it, and not say anything. If they fall off, they fall off, but it's bad if you say anything to them. (211)

Notice that Jessica has omitted quotation marks, indented the entire passage, used double spacing, and placed the citation outside the closing punctuation. She would start a new line (enter) for her discussion of the quotation.

© 2009. Teacher's Discovery®

Lead-ins from a Professional Writer

Lead-ins introduce the quoted material, providing smooth transitions and the full context of the quotation. Lead-ins often provide the credentials of the individual quoted, thus establishing his or her authority in the field. Careful writers utilize lead-ins to avoid repetitious use of "he saids" and "she writes," which are endemic to research papers. The following examples are taken from an article in the *Atlantic Monthly*, "Was the Great War Necessary?" by Benjamin Schwartz, in which the author reviews *The Pity of War* by Niall Ferguson. The discussion is about World War I. Note the variety of approaches that Schwartz uses to introduce quoted material.

Example

Moreover, as dreadful as was Britain's experience, "the disturbing paradox" of the Great War was, according to the historian J. M. Winter, that it was at once "an event of unparalleled carnage and suffering and the occasion of a significant improvement in the life expectancy of the civilian population…" (Schwartz 119).

In short, the goal was, in the words of the historian Imanuel Geiss, whom Ferguson quotes approvingly, "German leadership over a united Europe in order to brave the coming giant economic and political power blocs" (122).

Reviewing a war memoir in 1920, one critic plaintively sought some purpose behind the conflict: "Nowhere will you find a period or a sentence of which you could say, 'There! That is what we fought for!' The Cause finds no expression" (120).

Wilson stated his position clearly at the outset of his book: "Britain's involvement in the Great War was not some deplorable accident" (120).

As Ferguson acknowledges, Germany "forced the continental war of 1914 upon an unwilling France (and a not so unwilling Russia)" (122).

So they had come to believe, as the diplomat Sir Eyre Crowe put it, that "the building of the German fleet is but one of the symptoms of the disease. It is the political ambitions of the German Government and nation which are the source of the mischief" (123).

But those British generals, diplomats, and politicians . . . were hardly brimming with optimism—as Sir Edward Grey's oft-quoted lament, delivered on the eve of the war, attests: "The lamps are going out all over Europe; we shall not see them lit again in our lifetime" (128).

© 2009. Teacher's Discovery®

Providing Follow-ups of Direct Quotations

The main idea:

A direct quotation does not speak for itself. The writer usually must follow it up with explanation, discussion, or commentary instead of abandoning the quotation and letting it twist in the wind. Such commentary may focus on the significance of the quoted material, its implications, its relevance to the writer's argument, or its application to the topic under discussion. Follow-up sentences never paraphrase the quotation nor do they take the form *This quotation means …* or *The writer is saying …* Follow-up remarks add something worth saying to the discussion, often developing or amplifying the ideas the quotation expresses.

┌─**Example 1**───

Henry Kissinger writes:

> Over 540,000 American troops were fighting in Viet Nam, and our country was tearing itself apart over what Professor Walter A. McDougall of the University of Pennsylvania has brilliantly described as America's first "Great Society war." By this he meant that Viet Nam was the first American war fought for no military objective. Rather, the strategic goal was not to lose in order to give South Viet Nam time to create democratic institutions and social programs that would win the war for the hearts and minds of the population.

The author realizes that the reader may not understand the meaning of McDougall's phrase "Great Society war," so Kissinger provides an explanation. The follow-up is excellent because it clarifies an unfamiliar concept.

──

┌─**Example 2**───

Discussing H. D. Thoreau's unnerving visit to Mt. Katahdin in 1846, Bill Bryson writes:

> This wasn't the tame world of overgrown orchards and sun-dappled parks that passed for wilderness in suburban Concord, Massachusetts, but a forbidding, oppressive, primeval country that was "grim and wild … savage and dreary," fit only for "men nearer of kin to the rocks and wild animals than we." The experience left him, in the words of one biographer, "near hysterical." But even men far tougher and more attuned to the wilderness than Thoreau were sobered by its strange and palpable menace.

Bryson does not merely quote the words in Thoreau's description of the Maine wilderness. He goes beyond the quotation, providing more detail, and he adds that Thoreau's reaction, far from being unusual, was a common one at the time.

──

Example 3

Barbara Tuchman writes:

> Recognizing the prospect of siege, Cornwallis wrote Clinton as Commander-in-Chief on September 16-17, "If you cannot relieve me very soon, you must be prepared to hear the worst." The "worst" was left ambiguous. If the "worst" meant defeat or surrender, it must be inferred that Cornwallis, without a ready source of provisions, had no intention of fighting his way out by land.

Because the reader may not understand what *worst* means in this context, Tuchman explains what it means and what its implications were for the participants in this event. She provides a necessary amplification of the information in the quotation.

Example 4

Adam Hochschild writes:

> "Those who are conquered," wrote the philosopher Ibn Khaldun in the fourteenth-century, "always want to imitate the conqueror in his main characteristics—in his clothing, his crafts, and in all his distinctive traits and customs." Mobutu's luxurious Villa del Mare, a pink-and-white marble colonnaded chateau at Roquebrune-Cap-Martin on the French Riviera, complete with indoor and outdoor swimming pools, gold-fitted bathrooms, and heliport, lay a mere dozen miles down the coast from the estates Leopold once owned at Cap Ferrat.

Hochschild's follow-up provides specific details and examples that bring out the significance of the quotation. He shows the relevance of the 14th-century philosopher's statement by citing contemporary evidence and connecting it to his argument about the role of forced labor in colonial expansion.

Example 5

In an article about Richard Henry Dana, Castle Freeman Jr. writes:

> Reflecting on the great adventure of his youth and his life-long love of seafaring and distant lands, [Dana] wrote that he had been "lucky in travel, though in nothing else." He probably understood that he would be remembered, not for what he regarded as his real work, but for *Two Years before the Mast*, which he was apt to dismiss as "a boy's book" and regarded as the product of "a parenthesis in my life."

The quotation from Dana would have been confusing without Freeman's follow-up. He explains that the "lucky in travel" is a reference to the youthful adventures that led to Dana's famous book, while "in nothing else" alludes to his failure to achieve fame and success in his life's work: the law and public service. Freeman closes his short biographical piece with the above paragraph. It works because he has chosen his quotation from Dana wisely, and he has followed it up with the needed explanation.

© 2009. Teacher's Discovery®

Parenthetical Documentation

This section addresses parenthetical documentation, one of the most popular methods of showing, within the text of a paper, the exact information source, and giving credit to its author. It goes hand in hand with providing a complete list of the sources used (the works cited page or references page) and is an essential step in being a responsible user of information.

In Step 1, the section Using Resources Responsibly gives an overview of how to avoid plagiarism by providing five rules. Recall that, no matter what style of documentation, parenthetical documentation **must** be provided whenever

- using a direct quotation.
- paraphrasing—that is, restating in a personal way ideas or opinions that are not original thoughts.
- summarizing information or ideas using an individual writing style.

Documentation is not needed for an idea or information that is

- personal opinion, arrived at independently.
- common knowledge or an undisputed fact.

Both MLA and APA provide their own rules for how a researcher is to provide parenthetical documentation. Details for each follow.

Note:

Provide the source of a map, table, chart, graph, illustration, or diagram by placing the source information under the figure rather than in the text.

MLA Method

According to MLA, to provide parenthetical documentation, give the source (usually just the author's last name and the page number) within parentheses after the borrowed material in a paper. If the source consists of only one page of text, no page number is required. Electronic publications are tricky, as many do not have pagination. Do not use the page number generated by a printer if the original document does not include page numbers. Use a paragraph number only if it is provided in the original document—i.e. (Smith par. 4). If the source does not include any of these organizational options, then refer only to the author's last name.

Example

> During the Middle Ages, people thought of the labyrinth in art as something enjoyable, exemplifying both God's creation and human artistry (Doob 144).

The parenthetical citation—(Doob 144)—shows that the information about this view of labyrinths comes from page number 144 of a book by Doob. The works cited page at the end of a paper will provide complete publication information about this book. For example:

Works cited entry

> Doob, Penelope Reed. *The Idea of the Labyrinth from Classical Antiquity through the Middle Ages.* Ithaca: Cornell UP, 1990. Print.

© 2009. Teacher's Discovery®

MLA General Guidelines for Parenthetical Documentation

General Rules and Examples

Guide 1. The information in **parenthetical citations** must match the corresponding information on the **works cited** page.

Guide 2. The parenthetical citation usually appears **at the end of the sentence**, as close as possible to the material it documents, so that it does not interrupt the flow of the writing.

Guide 3. To cite an entire work, include the author's name within the paper's text.

Example

> Abdel Bari Atwan gives an overview of the origin, growth and development of the terrorist
>
> organization in his book *The Secret History of al Qaeda*.

No parenthetical citation follows, but complete information appears on the works cited page.

Works cited entry

> Atwan, Abdel Bari. *The Secret History of al Qaeda*. Berkeley: U of California P, 2006.

Guide 4. If the author's name appears in a sentence of the paper, then do not repeat it in the citation:

Example

> Orwell made this point earlier in "Shooting an Elephant" (65-66).

Guide 5. If citing the same author twice in a row, omit the author's name in the second citation, using the page number only. However, when citing a different author in between, include the author's name again in the second citation:

Example

> He accepts a sad truth: "History is made by warfare, greed, lust for power, hatred, and xenophobia…"
>
> (Gould 280). But he wishes to argue that aggressiveness and selfishness by no means define the
>
> human being. On the contrary, one must factor in the "ten thousand ordinary acts of kindness" that
>
> characterize human experience (282).

> He accepts a sad truth: "History is made by warfare, greed, lust for power, hatred, and xenophobia…"
>
> (Gould 280). But he wishes to argue that aggressiveness and selfishness by no means define the
>
> human being. On the contrary, concern for others appeared early in human history, as exemplified
>
> by the Neanderthals' practice of caring for their sick (Diamond 38). One must factor in the "ten
>
> thousand ordinary acts of kindness" that characterize human experience (Gould 282), rather than
>
> assuming that our tendency toward violence is a biological necessity.

© 2009. Teacher's Discovery®

Guide 6. Make parenthetical citations **brief** and use as **few** as clarity and accuracy permit. Give only the essential information, and do not add parenthetical references unnecessarily.

Guide 7. The parenthetical citation normally **precedes the punctuation mark** that concludes the sentence, clause, or phrase containing the borrowed material.

┌─**Example**───

> In his essay on cannibals, Montaigne mentions the disappearance of the great island of Atlantis
>
> (138-140).

Guide 8. If a direct quotation occurs **at the end of the sentence**, insert the parenthetical citation between the closing quotation mark and the concluding punctuation mark.

┌─**Example**───

> He concludes his review of Anne Tyler's latest book with the declaration, "This writer is not merely
>
> good, she is wickedly good" (Updike 278).

Guide 9. In an extended quotation of **more than four typed lines**, which is indented one inch (or ten spaces) and is typed double-spaced, the citation follows the last line of the quotation and is placed outside the ending punctuation.

┌─**Example**───

> In *A Distant Mirror*, Barbara Tuchman alludes to the traditional personification of Death:
>
> > A skeleton with hourglass and scythe, in a white shroud or bare-boned, grinning at the irony of
> >
> > man's fate reflected in his image: that all men, from beggar to emperor, from harlot to queen,
> >
> > from ragged clerk to Pope, must come to this. No matter what their poverty or power in life, all
> >
> > is vanity, equalized in death. (124)

© 2009. Teacher's Discovery®

MLA Specific Guides for Parenthetical Documentations

Guide 1.   In a paper based on a **single primary source**, for example, a novel, play, or poem, most teachers are satisfied if a page number or line number in parentheses follows the material to which it refers.

> ─**Example** ─────────────────────────────────
> In a paper citing only *The Catcher in the Rye*, a citation would look like this:
>
> > After watching Phoebe riding on the carousel, Holden realizes that adults must let children take
> >
> > chances. He concludes, "If they fall off, they fall off, but it's bad if you say anything to them" (211).

Guide 2.   If a works cited list contains **only one source by one author**, give only the author's last name: (Morgan 210).

Guide 3.   If a works cited list contains sources by **two authors with the same last name**, include the first initial of the author cited: (P. Morgan 42-44) for Percy and (R. Morgan 176) for Regina.

Guide 4.   If there are two P. Morgans—Peter and Paula, for example—then it is necessary to include the entire first name for each: (Peter Morgan 65) and (Paula Morgan 119).

Guide 5.   If one work has **two to three authors**, include the last name of each: (Hart, Schafner, and Marx 35).

Guide 6.   If one work has **three or more authors**, use the last name of the first author, followed by et al., with no intervening punctuation: (Williams et al. 109-112).

Guide 7.   If a work has a **corporate author**, e.g., Government Printing Office or American Library Association, use that name, shortened if possible: (GPO 89) and (ALA 356-360).

Guide 8.   If a work is listed by **its title only**, use the title, shortened if possible: (*Guidelines*) and ("Pelican").

Guide 9.   If the works cited list contains **more than one work by an author**, give the title, shortened if possible, with a comma only between the author's name and the work: (Chin, *History* 435) and (Chin, *Dragons* 67).

Guide 10.   If citing a **multivolume work**, give volume as well as page number(s), placing a colon between volume and page number: (Hume 4: 400-407).

   The citation for an entire volume looks like this: (Schlesinger, vol. 4).

Guide 11.   The citation for a classic literary work—for example, *To the Lighthouse*, by Virginia Woolf—may also include chapter numbers so that readers using a different edition than the one cited may find the relevant material. Give the page number first, followed by a semicolon, and then the chapter, using appropriate abbreviations: (Woolf 195; chap. 2) and (273; chap. 3).

© 2009. Teacher's Discovery®

Guide 12. In citations for classic verse plays and poems, omit page numbers and cite by division (act, scene, canto, book, part) and line. Use periods to separate these numbers. To cite act 5, scene 1, line 101 in *Hamlet*, write: (*Hamlet* 5.1.101).

To cite lines in canto 17 of Dante's *Inferno*, write: (*Inferno* 17.1-26).

Guide 13. Citations for the Bible and other religious works omit page numbers but include book, chapter, and line numbers. (Exod. 14.19-25).

A citation for sura 54 of the Koran would read: (Koran 54.33-55).

Guide 14. When citing electronic sources, give the author's name and page number or paragraph number, if available. (Gordon par. 25).

Guide 15. If the source lacks numbering, omit numbers from the parenthetical references. Do not include the page numbers of a printout from the Web since these may vary. (Martindale).

Guide 16. Omit page numbers in citations of entire works, encyclopedia articles, non-print sources, or one-page works.

Guide 17. Combine **two sources in one citation** where appropriate; separating them with a semi-colon: (Tinker 48; Evers 90) and (Evers 129; Chance 74).

APA Method

To provide parenthetical documentation, use the author–date method of citation, that is, give the surname of the author and the year of publication, inserted in the text at the appropriate point.

Example

> Many young auto thieves described their motivation to steal as the desire for thrills and excitement, including the fun of police chases, rather than the urge to make money (Copes, 2003).

The citation—(Copes, 2003)—shows that the information about this type of street crime comes from an article by Copes that appeared in 2003. The references page at the end of the paper will provide the complete publication information.

Reference page entry

> Copes, H. (2003). Streetlife and the rewards of auto theft. *Deviant Behavior*, 24, 309-332.

APA General Guidelines for Reference Citations Within Text

Guide 1. The information in reference citations in the text must match the corresponding information in the **reference list.**

Guide 2. The reference citation is inserted in **mid-sentence**, or **at the end of the sentence**, as close as possible to the material it documents.

Guide 3. If the author's name appears in a sentence of the paper, do **not** repeat it in the citation.

> ┌─ **Example** ─────────────────────────────────────
>
> Dittmar, Halliwell, and Stirling (2009) observed that advertisements featuring thin models did not
>
> adversely affect the body image of all women.

Guide 4. Make reference citations **brief** and use as **few** as clarity and accuracy permit. Give only the required information, and do not add parenthetical references unnecessarily.

Guide 5. The reference citation at the end of a sentence **precedes the punctuation mark** that concludes the sentence, clause, or phrase containing the borrowed material.

> ┌─ **Example** ─────────────────────────────────────
>
> Pathological game-playing behavior is linked to lower scholastic performance and attention
>
> problems (Gentile, 2009).

Guide 6. If a direct quotation occurs **at the end of the sentence**, insert the reference citation between the closing quotation mark and the concluding punctuation mark.

> ┌─ **Example** ─────────────────────────────────────
>
> Gilmore describes this study as a response to "the phenomenal growth of the California prison
>
> population since 1982" (Haslam, 2008, p. 468).

Guide 7. An extended quotation of **more than 40 words** is known as a **block quotation**. It is indented five spaces and is typed double-spaced, without quotation marks. The citation follows the last word of the quotation and is placed outside the ending punctuation.

> ┌─ **Example** ─────────────────────────────────────
>
> Muller, Gudrow, and Schneider (2009) attempt to explain the difference between these results and the
>
> results found in a similar survey (Carter & Ross, 2006):
>
> > The inclusion of female body builders in the current study may have increased the percentage of women
> >
> > who reported the use of size-enhancing supplements, thereby eliminating the gender differences in
> >
> > regards to this behavior. This finding does, however, lend support to the idea that the behavior of female
> >
> > athletes is changing and in many ways is becoming very similar to the behavior of male athletes. (p. 513)

© 2009. Teacher's Discovery®

APA Additional Guides to Reference Citation Within Text

Guide 1. If a reference list contains only one work by one author, give only the date, or the author's last name and the date.

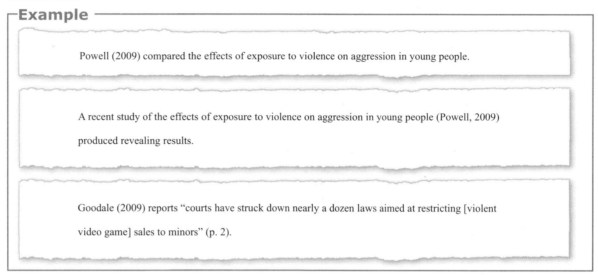

┌─**Example**───

> Powell (2009) compared the effects of exposure to violence on aggression in young people.

> A recent study of the effects of exposure to violence on aggression in young people (Powell, 2009) produced revealing results.

> Goodale (2009) reports "courts have struck down nearly a dozen laws aimed at restricting [violent video game] sales to minors" (p. 2).

Guide 2. If a list contains **two primary authors with the same surname**, include the first author's initials in all text citations, even if the year of publication differs.

┌─**Example**───

> J.S. Clark (2008) and M. Clark (2005) also studied this effect.

Guide 3. If one work has **two authors**, always cite both names every time a reference occurs in the text: … (Trout & Christie, 2007) ….

Guide 4. If one work has **three, four, or five authors**, cite all authors the first time a reference occurs; in subsequent citations, include only the surname of the first author followed by "et al." (un-italicized and followed by a period) then the year if it is the first reference within a paragraph.

First citation: … Barendregt, Bekker, and Baauw (2008) found …

Subsequent to first citation per paragraph: … Barendregt et al. (2008) found …

Omit date from subsequent citations per paragraph: … Barendregt et al. found …

Guide 5. When a work has **six or more authors**, cite only the surname of the first author followed by "et al." (un-italicized and followed by a period) then the year for the first and subsequent citations: … Gentile et al. (2009) also found …

If two references with six or more authors shorten to the same form, cite the surnames of the first authors and as many subsequent authors as necessary to distinguish the two references.

© 2009. Teacher's Discovery®

Guide 6.   If the work has a **group as author**, e.g., corporations, associations, government agencies, and study groups, the names are usually spelled out each time they appear in a text citation. The names of some group authors are spelled out the first time and abbreviated thereafter.

First text citation: …(National Institute of Mental Health [NIMH], 2009) …

Subsequent to first citation per paragraph: … (NIMH, 2009) …

Guide 7.   If the work **has no author**, cite within the text the first few words of the reference list entry (usually the title) and the year. Use double quotation marks around the title of an article or chapter, and italicize the title of a periodical, book, brochure, or report.

… on managed care ("Study Finds," 2008) ….

… the book *Community Service Opportunities* (2009) ….

If the work's author is designated as Anonymous, cite in text the word Anonymous, followed by a comma and the date: … (Anonymous, 2009) ….

Guide 8.   When **two or more works are cited within the same parentheses, arrange them** in the same order in which they appear in the reference list and separate them with a semi-colon. If two or more works by the same author or authors are cited in the same parentheses, list the name only once and follow with the year of publication, earliest to latest.

Past research (Reed, 2009; Royale & Smith, 2005) suggests a similar conclusion.

Past research (Garcia, 1999, 2004) suggests a similar conclusion.

Guide 9.   If the list contains **more than one work by the same author** (or by the same two or more authors in the same order) with the same publication date, identify the works by the suffixes a, b, c, and so forth after the year; repeat the year.

Several studies (Fitzmartin & Jacobsen, 1998a, 1998b, 1998c; Rishi, 2001a, 2008b) support this view.

Guide 10.   To cite specific parts of a source, give the page, chapter, figure, table, or equation at the appropriate place in the text. For quotations, always provide page numbers. Page and chapter are abbreviated in in-text citations as follows:

(Davies, 2008, p. 4) and (Wicks-Nelson & Israel, 2009, chap. 5)

Guide 11.   To cite **specific parts of an electronic** source where no page numbers are provided, use the paragraph number, if available, preceded by the abbreviation para. If neither paragraph nor page numbers are visible, cite the heading and the number of the paragraph following it.

As Mingus (2001, para.4) points out, and (Bloch, 2001, Conclusion section, para. 3)

Guide 12.   **Personal communications** may be letters, memos, some electronic communications (e.g., e-mail, messages from non-archived discussion groups or electronic bulletin boards), personal interviews, telephone conversations, and the like. Do not include them in the reference list; cite them in the text only. Give the initials as well as the surname of the communicator, and provide as exact a date as possible.

W. P. Mui (personal communication, February 7, 2009)

Guide 13.   In **citations in parenthetical material**, use commas, not brackets, to set off the date.

(see Table 2 of Weed, Saunders, & Wright, 1998, for complete data)

© 2009. Teacher's Discovery®

Step 7 Summary

Using Borrowed Material:

- Paraphrase or summarize most borrowed material; use direct quotations sparingly.

- Clarify and simplify while restating the essential ideas, facts, and conclusions of the original.

- Condense lengthy excerpts by omitting descriptive details, examples, quotations, and repetition.

- Choose direct quotations wisely, based on relevance, grace of expression, and aptness.

- Always introduce a direct quotation by identifying the speaker, mentioning a cited authority's credentials, or providing the context. **Never** insert a direct quotation without an introductory phrase. **Never, ever**.

- Make sure quotes are exact, including spelling and punctuation. Use ellipses to show omissions; avoid quoting long passages.

- Follow up a direct quotation with an explanation, commentary, or clarification, as appropriate. Do not assume that the quotation can stand by itself. It can't.

Parenthetical Documentation:

- Parenthetical citations are required for all borrowed material, whether paraphrased, summarized, or quoted directly. Maps, charts, diagrams, and the like also require source information.

- Follow formatting guidelines exactly, and enclose the citation in parentheses.

- Keep parenthetical citations brief and use as few as accuracy permits.

- Make sure that in-text citations match **exactly** the corresponding information on the **works cited page** or **references page**.

© 2009. Teacher's Discovery®

Step 8

Writing the Rough Draft

Special Considerations for Empirical Studies in the Sciences

Drafting the Paper

Writing the Introduction and Conclusion

© 2009. Teacher's Discovery®

This step provides help for the next step—to begin drafting a paper. The major task is moving borrowed material recorded on note cards into the paper itself, keeping in mind that accuracy, honesty, and the inclusion of analysis and insight are all crucial.

A quick review of the most recent steps shows what has been gathered so far.

The student has

- revised the thesis statement as research has progressed.
- accurately copied information onto note cards.
- sorted note cards into piles according to topic headings and set aside or discarded irrelevant cards.
- updated the outline, briefly noting the information collected during note taking and assigning it to the major supporting topics.

Warning: Some dead ends and traps to avoid:

 Inadequate paraphrasing and faulty documentation can lead to plagiarism.

 Sloppy presentation of borrowed material can misrepresent an author's original point of view.

 Using direct quotations without introduction or segue leads to sloppy or confusing papers.

 Long lists of quotations without adequate follow-up discussion or explanation create potential confusion for the reader.

Before putting pen to paper (so to speak), consider the type of paper that is assigned, being sure there is a clear understanding of form and format. Science research reports, in particular, often require a specific format that helps guide organization and composition.

© 2009. Teacher's Discovery®

Special Considerations for Empirical Studies in the Sciences

Some science reports, particularly those in which collected data from research and experimentation are presented, follow specific formatting guidelines. These guidelines may conform to a teacher's instructions or a published style. In general, science reports follow the IMRAD model: introduction, methods, results, and discussion, as well as an abstract and a list of references. Described is the IMRAD model for science writing.

Title   The title of the report should be as specific as possible, clearly describing what has been studied. Do not include words such as "an investigation into …" or "a study on …"

> **Example**
>
> The Association of Tuberculosis with HIV Infection in Ethiopia in 2007

Abstract   The abstract is a condensed version of the paper. In one paragraph, summarize the research by stating the main objectives of the experiment (or what the experiment is designed to reveal), describing the methods of experimentation, summarizing the most important findings, and stating the major conclusions. A good way to compose the abstract is to write a sentence or two that summarizes the main points from each of the sections in the paper. This method ensures that information provided in the abstract follows the same order and emphasis of the research. Although this is the first section of the paper, write it last so that it accurately reflects the contents of the paper.

Introduction   Identify the issue(s) studied and describe previous research conducted in this area, citing all sources correctly. Follow the review of previous literature with an explanation of how this study will enhance, extend, or clarify the previous research.

The introduction should end with a purpose statement, which states the specific issue that will be addressed by this particular experiment.

Methods   Describe, in a narrative way, how the experiment is set up and conducted. Describe the materials or subjects used and each step of the experiment. Provide enough detail to enable others to replicate the experiment. This section generally uses past tense and passive voice.

 Note:

Any methods borrowed from other researchers should be cited.

Results   Report experiment results, or what is observed. Do not include interpretation of these results. Whenever possible, use tables, graphs, and charts to show what data was collected. Use past tense.

Discussion   Interpret the results by summarizing the most important findings first, then explaining the patterns or principles illustrated. Compare personal findings to the results of the studies cited in the introduction. Again, cite the studies in this section, and explain any contradictions and/or any agreements in findings. Finally, extend the discussion to explore the wider implications or meanings of the personal findings.

References   Use the APA guidelines to cite all sources used in the paper.

© 2009. Teacher's Discovery®

Drafting the Paper

Procedure for Moving From Note Cards to Rough Draft

Task 1.   Arrange all note cards for the first body section of the paper in the order that they will be used, then number the cards in the upper left corner. Work on one section of the paper at a time.

Task 2.   Write the **topic sentence** for the first body section, using the topic sentence from the expanded outline, improving on the phrasing, if possible. Make sure this sentence introduces the main idea planned for development in this section. When necessary, use additional sentences to make the idea clear.

Task 3.   Begin providing **support for that idea**, the first major supporting topic, using the information from the cards in their predetermined order.

Task 4.   Remember to use borrowed material in up to three different ways: **paraphrasing, summarizing,** and **quoting directly**.

Task 5.   Insert parenthetical citations (e.g., Levinson 47) **as the writing progresses**. Do not even think about adding them later! **It's a "cite as you write" process.**

Task 6.   Remember that a direct quotation always requires a lead-in—that is to say, words and phrases need to introduce the quote.

Example

Direct quotations are never rudely inserted; they follow such phrases as these:

> According to Secretary of State Hillary Clinton, "The United States is fully engaged and ready to lead …"

> As *Boston Globe* columnist Cathy Young points out, "Gulag revisionism is not stigmatized the way Holocaust revisionism is."

> Ezra Pound, one of the most famous and controversial poets of the 20th-century, observes, "Literature is language charged with meaning."

Note:

Keep the following rule in mind:

L-I   **Lead-In using introductory words and phrases**

Q   **Quote accurately**

F-U   **Follow Up with comments and explanation**

© 2009. Teacher's Discovery®

Task 7. Continue importing the information from the note cards into the paper, introducing and citing as it moves along, until adequate support has been provided for this particular topic.

Always provide commentary and discussion of borrowed materials. Some students find it easier to put the borrowed materials into the paper first, and then expand discussion of the researched information in the next task. This section should now look like Meg's draft on page 101.

Task 8. With note cards numbered in their order of use, highlight the material from each note card that appears in the paper. Put the number of the corresponding note card in the right margin of the paper. Highlighting the borrowed material makes it apparent whether this material is being used appropriately, as well as whether the student has provided adequate interpretation and analysis. The draft will now resemble the second version of Meg's paper, on page 101.

Task 9. Check the highlighted material, including the in-text citations, for accuracy, and make the needed corrections.

Now, go through the first body section carefully, noting where to add more follow-up comments, explanations, discussion, interpretation, and evaluations of borrowed material. Without the addition of personal ideas, a paper is a patchwork of borrowed material, not a superior research paper. Review all personal comments and questions that have been recorded on the note cards to see that they have been addressed.

Note:

YOU are the owner of this paper, YOU are presenting material to support a statement formulated by YOU, and one YOU consider worth saying. Borrowed material helps support YOUR idea, but YOU also need to explain how and why it does this.

Look at Meg's revised paragraph on page 102.

Task 10. With each review of the first body section, try to improve upon the wording, sentence combinations, and overall clarity of thought.

Provide transitions for smoothness and coherence. Words like *however, therefore, nonetheless,* etc., provide connections between ideas and guide the reader through the logic of the argument. Transitions can also take the form of phrases, where information from a previous sentence or paragraph is reiterated and used to compare or contrast a new idea.

Task 11. Repeat this process for the remaining body sections.

Keep all material (source cards, outlines, note cards, and separate drafts of the paper) in one safe place. Paper clips, rubber bands, and large envelopes are all helpful for keeping information together and preventing material from getting lost. Save computer files in more than place (back up to another PC, flashdrive, or other storage media), especially when using school computers. It's a good idea to email a copy of the latest draft to oneself, so if the hard drive crashes or the flash drive is lost, the work is still retrievable. There are also free online data storage sites that make it easy to work from anywhere.

© 2009. Teacher's Discovery®

Now let's follow a student through this process.

Example: Meg's Note Cards

Meg's thesis statement: To become the first female Justice on the Supreme Court, Sandra Day O'Connor had to overcome many obstacles with hard work and determination.

Meg's topic headings: Childhood and Education, Major Professional Accomplishments, and Contributions to the Supreme Court.

Meg's note cards about O'Connor's early life look like this:

Childhood and Education   *Biskupec 20*

[O'Connor's] version of events reveals a series of episodes in which she tries desperately to prove herself. She would paint a screen door over and over until it was exactly to her father's specifications.

Card 1

Childhood and Education   *Rosen 32*

[Brother Alan] Day, who ran the family ranch for many years, says that his sister's upbringing as a rancher made her independent and self-reliant. "You would be out on the ranch in a pickup or on horseback, or whatever," he relates, "when you would come upon a situation that needed a response: a broken fence or a windmill or a sick cow or a flat tire or a broken fan belt. There wasn't anybody to call and there wasn't anybody to take care of you. You very quickly learned that you're responsible for yourself."

Card 2

Childhood and Education   *Biskupec 23*

[At Stanford] she was an enthusiastic and adroit competitor who loved all manner of sports and games. Her worries about fitting in were dissolving into successes as she took advantage of the opportunities presented to her by Stanford.

Card 3

Childhood and Education   *Marie 42*

Growing up on the sprawling "Lazy B" ranch in harsh, sun-baked southeastern Arizona made her life more of a challenge...For entertainment, the young Sandra Day would ride horses and read. She also learned to drive a car on the ranch at age seven and could handle a truck and a tractor at ten.

Card 4

© 2009. Teacher's Discovery®

Example: Meg's First Draft

The **first version** of Meg's paragraph looks like this:

> Even when she was extremely young, Sandra Day O'Connor showed the qualities that would later help her achieve appointment as the first female Supreme Court Justice. Growing up on a remote Arizona ranch, she faced many challenges and had learned to drive a car as well as a tractor before she was even ten years old (Marie 42). Her brother, Alan Day, believed that growing up on the ranch allowed O'Connor to develop independence and self-reliance. He recollected that the realities of ranch life often included situations, like getting a flat tire or finding a sick cow, that required immediate attention. He said that in these circumstances, "There wasn't anyone to call and there wasn't anybody to take care of you. You very quickly learned that you are responsible for yourself" (Rosen 32). Her father's high expectations also made O'Connor feel like she had to prove herself, which in one case resulted in her repainting a door many times until he was satisfied (Biskupec 20). When O'Connor was 16, she left her family to attend Stanford University in California. There, she was described by her biographer Joan Biskupec as "an enthusiastic and adroit competitor who loved all manner of sports and games" (23).

See how Meg has taken the accurately recorded borrowed material as it appears on her note cards and woven it into her rough draft through direct quotation, paraphrasing, and summary. The parenthetical citations provide the documentation, showing the exact source of each piece of information.

Notice that, if she used the author's name in the text, she lists only the page number in the citation.

Example: Meg's Second Draft

The **second version** of Meg's paragraph looks like this. She has highlighted all borrowed material and shown from which card it comes. This makes it easy to see that the paragraph is almost entirely borrowed material, with no contributions from the author.

> Even when she was extremely young, Sandra Day O'Connor showed the qualities that would later help her achieve appointment as the first female Supreme Court Justice. Growing up on a remote ranch in Arizona, she faced many challenges and had learned to drive a car as well as a tractor before she was even ten years old (Marie 42). Her brother, Alan Day, believed that growing up on the ranch allowed O'Connor to develop independence and self-reliance. He recollected that the realities of ranch life often included situations, like getting a flat tire or finding a sick cow, that required immediate attention. He said that in those circumstances, "There wasn't anyone to call and there wasn't anybody to take care of you. You very quickly learned that you are responsible for yourself" (Rosen 32). Her father's high expectations also made O'Connor feel like she had to prove herself, which in one case resulted in her repainting a door many times until he was satisfied (Biskupec 20). When O'Connor was 16, she left her family to attend Stanford University in California. There, she was described by her biographer Joan Biskupec as "an enthusiastic and adroit competitor who 3 loved all manner of sports and games" (23).

— 4
— 2
— 1
— 3

© 2009. Teacher's Discovery®

Example: Meg's Third Draft

Below is Meg's **third version**. She added supplementary material of her own, including comments, explanations, and discussion of the borrowed material. This new material is underlined to show how to add personal interpretations, comments, and discussion. Without these additions, Meg's example paragraph would be primarily quoted material rather than a promising start to her essay.[12]

Even when she was extremely young, Sandra Day O'Connor showed the qualities that would later see her installed as the first female Supreme Court Justice. Growing up on a remote Arizona ranch, she faced many challenges and had learned to drive a car as well as a tractor before she was even ten years old (Marie 42). Instead of playing as other children did, she took part in activities that are often considered "adult" tasks, and which at that time were also often reserved for men. Her brother, Alan Day, believed that growing up on the ranch allowed O'Connor to develop independence and self-reliance. He recollected that the realities of ranch life often included situations, like getting a flat tire or finding a sick cow, that required immediate attention. He said that in these circumstances, "There wasn't anyone to call and there wasn't anybody to take care of you. You very quickly learned that you are responsible for yourself" (Rosen 32). In addition to having to learn adult skills and deal independently with problems, O'Connor felt that she had to live up to her father's exacting standards. In one incident she had to repaint a door many times until he was satisfied (Biskupec 20). While these experiences must have been difficult at times, they probably also gave O'Connor determination to accomplish tasks as well as confidence in her own abilities. These traits led her to Stanford University when she was 16 years old. There, she was described by her biographer Joan Biskupec as "an enthusiastic and adroit competitor who loved all manner of sports and games" (23). Participating in competitive sports likely complemented O'Connor's qualities of self-reliance and determination by giving her the opportunity to test herself against other people. All of these traits, developed during her childhood and adolescence, contributed to her singular strength of character that later allowed her to break gender barriers and become one of the most important women in America.

---

[12] The borrowed material in this example is from the following:

Biskupic, Joan. *Sandra Day O'Connor: How the First Woman on the Supreme Court Became Its Most Influential Justice.* New York: Harper, 2005. Print.

Marie, Joan S. "Her Honor: The Rancher's Daughter." *Saturday Evening Post 257* (Sept 1985): 42(7). *Student Resource Center - Gold.* Gale.

Rosen, Jeffrey. "A Majority of One." *The New York Times Magazine* June 3, 2001: 32. *Student Resource Center - Gold.* Gale.

© 2009. Teacher's Discovery®

Writing the Introduction and Conclusion

Now that all of the body sections are composed in the paper's first draft, the paper needs an introduction and conclusion. Just as with the body sections, these can be improved upon as the whole paper is polished in Step 9. However, formulating the introduction and conclusion into prose is what's important here. From an inviting start to a satisfying close, this portion of Step 8 explains how to write the introductory and concluding paragraphs.

The Introduction

There are many ways to begin. Regardless of which approach is chosen, the introductory paragraphs of a research paper usually include the following three elements:

Element 1. Focusing sentences

- direct the reader's attention to the topic of the paper.

- are sometimes called the **grabbers**, because their purpose is to grab the reader's attention.

- should not be painfully obvious or trite generalizations. Starting with *Albert Einstein was a great scientist* or *Life has its ups and downs* will induce instant sleep in a reader. Dictionary definitions are also stunningly boring.

- should consist of several thought-provoking, original sentences that draw the reader into the discussion.

Element 2. A thesis statement

- is the carefully worded statement of the main idea of the paper; never begins, *In this paper I will …*

- almost always includes a judgment or evaluation; is never merely a statement of fact.

- may come right after the focusing sentences, or may come near the end of the thesis paragraph.

Element 3. The method of development (MOD)

- is a **brief** indication of the main topics that the author will use to support the thesis statement, like a blueprint.

- is the writer's own work, containing nothing borrowed.

- is usually followed by several additional sentences to bring the introductory paragraph(s) to a satisfactory close.

Experienced writers include these three elements in their opening paragraphs. A good introductory paragraph does more, however: it establishes a tone, making efforts to engage the reader's attention from the outset. A few of the techniques used to achieve this goal are listed below.

© 2009. Teacher's Discovery®

Techniques to add zip to an introduction.

- An entertaining anecdote, story, conversation, or example
- A strong, controversial opinion that opposes common assumptions or critical views
- An unusual or startling fact; surprising statistics or data
- A witty or humorous observation, if appropriate for the subject under discussion
- A dramatic, fascinating quotation, adage, or proverb

Examples of Well-formed Introductory Paragraphs

In the following examples, note how each student includes the important elements of the introduction while creating an engaging tone. Thesis statements have been highlighted.

Example: Brian on Ernest Hemingway

In this introductory paragraph, Brian explains that his paper will trace author Ernest Hemingway's major influences.

> Although an author's work should not be evaluated primarily through the lens of his or her biography, many different influences can affect a writer's development. In the case of Ernest Hemingway, although his experience as a reporter helped shape his style, other authors and their work exerted the major influence on Hemingway's work as a whole. His early writing owes much to several American authors, most notably, Sherwood Anderson. Mark Twain, whom Hemingway admired greatly, was also influential. And Gertrude Stein's ruthless criticism of his manuscripts helped him to write more succinctly. In the end, the Nobel Laureate owed many debts to both his predecessors and his contemporaries.

Example: Juan on Marie Curie

To begin his biographical paper on Marie Curie, Juan introduces the idea that Curie overcame many formidable obstacles before becoming a world-famous, award-winning scientist.

> Throughout history, it has been difficult for women to achieve world renown. This is especially true, until recently, in fields such as mathematics and science. But Marie Curie, who lived from 1867 to 1934, won acclaim for her discoveries in chemistry and physics. She struggled against poverty and discrimination to obtain an excellent education, and then through years of hard work, she made important contributions to her field. Twice honored with the Nobel Prize, she is one of the most important women in the history of science.

© 2009. Teacher's Discovery®

Example: Ava on Censorship

For a paper arguing against the censorship of a controversial book, Ava provides an overview of the debate and a clear statement of her argument.

> In writing children's literature, authors beg a difficult favor of parents. Beyond asking the opportunity to entertain or educate children, these writers seek access to the ultimate artistic medium: a forming mind. Ideas and perspectives that books introduce to young readers can have immeasurable impact, a fact that requires competent parents and schools to scrutinize children's books before presenting them to impressionable readers. School officials, at the same time, have a responsibility to recognize the value in certain works, despite the controversy they inspire. *Revolting Rhymes* by Roald Dahl is such a book. Although the macabre poems of Dahl's collection may not be appropriate for children in elementary school, educators should permit older students to read the book.

Example: Rick on Roller Coasters

This introductory paragraph is from Rick's informative speech on the popularity of roller coasters. It uses concrete detail and specific information to take the audience to the main question that the speech addresses: Why are roller coasters so immensely popular?

> From Cedar Point Park in Sandusky, Ohio, to Busch Gardens in Williamsburg, Virginia, the roller coaster dominates the scene. Whether it is the shuttle loop of the Viper at Six Flags Over Georgia, or the mildly tot-terrorizing Kiddie Coaster at Playland in Rye, New York, the roller coaster has been the star attraction at amusement parks since 1886. The success of this ride is no accident. It took years of experimentation and constant improvement to build roller coasters that would provide maximum thrills without endangering lives. Today the coaster's overwhelming popularity in amusement parks around the world is the result of ingenious design, engineering skill, and the application of psychology.

Notice that Rick has combined his thesis statement and MOD, an acceptable practice as long as the resulting sentence does not become too long and confusing.

© 2009. Teacher's Discovery®

The Conclusion

The concluding paragraphs of a paper bring the paper to a satisfactory close. The concluding paragraph should include these four elements:

Element 1. Sentences to refocus attention and signal the end of the paper.

Element 2. A reworded thesis statement—not a word-for-word repetition—as a reminder of the main idea of the paper—that is, a judgment, decision, argument, resolution, or the like.

Element 3. A recapitulation—a concise summary of the major topics covered.

Element 4. Sentences that go beyond the conclusion of the thesis, often by doing one of the following:

- providing a new insight or perspective.

- suggesting logical implications or practical consequences of the position stated.

- challenging the reader to take action or change behavior through specific proposals.

- showing how this view or discovery fits into the larger picture.

- making a prediction about future developments in this particular field.

- raising additional questions about the topic or suggesting the direction that future investigation might take.

- mentioning a noteworthy incident, surprising statistic, apt quotation, or striking contrast that reinforces the main point of the essay.

- offering a personal reflection.

A good conclusion

 leaves the reader with a strong impression, a definite attitude.

 is the author's own work and does not contain much, if any, borrowed material. A brief, highly appropriate quotation, a statistic, or an anecdote can be included when it reflects and extends the ideas that have already been fully developed in the body of the paper.

 reflects the introduction by alluding to the same idea, saying, anecdote, or incident mentioned earlier.

 does NOT merely repeat.

 does NOT begin "In conclusion" or "Finally." All but the dimmest reader can see that the end is in sight.

© 2009. Teacher's Discovery®

Examples of Well-formed Conclusion Paragraphs

Example: Brian's conclusion for Hemingway

Ernest Hemingway's mature style reflects his experience as a journalist as well as his admiration for such writers as Sherwood Anderson, Stephen Crane, and Mark Twain. It also shows the influence of Gertrude Stein, who for a brief time was Hemingway's mentor and critic. Yet despite these influences, Hemingway developed and perfected his own style, and in the end, distanced himself from other American writers. In terms of both style and content, he was truly his own person. His many excellent short stories and his finest novels continue the tradition of American literature and also make an original contribution to it.

Example: Juan's conclusion for Marie Curie

Throughout her education and career in physics and chemistry, Marie Curie showed the determination and willingness to work hard that made her a world class scientist. Her work in radioactivity and her discovery of several elements won her fame and culminated in the highest honors that a scientist can win. In the years following Curie's first Nobel Prize in 1903, only nine other women have become Nobel Laureates in science, further evidence of the extraordinary nature of her achievement. Decades after her death in 1934, Curie still provides inspiration to those who pursue scientific truth, and especially to women.

Example: Ava's conclusion on censorship

There is little doubt that *Revolting Rhymes* is unsuitable for elementary school children. In producing such a grotesque collection of poems and pictures, Roald Dahl and Quentin Blake compromised a portion of their potential audience. However, the book's offending feature, Dahl's biting, sardonic humor, is precisely what endears *Revolting Rhymes* to older children. In concentrating their efforts on a specific age group, both writer and illustrator establish a unique connection with their young readers and intensify the effect of their art. *Revolting Rhymes*, unrepentant vulgarity and all, thrills its target audience in a way that no inoffensive, antiseptic storybook could.

© 2009. Teacher's Discovery®

Practice Composing a Conclusion

Look again at Rick's introductory paragraph below, followed by suggestions for writing strong conclusions.

> From Cedar Point Park in Sandusky, Ohio, to Busch Gardens in Williamsburg, Virginia, the roller coaster dominates the scene. Whether it is the shuttle loop of the Viper at Six Flags Over Georgia, or the mildly tot-terrorizing Kiddie Coaster at Playland in Rye, New York, the roller coaster has been the star attraction at amusement parks since 1886. The success of this ride is no accident. It took years of experimentation and constant improvement to build roller coasters that would provide maximum thrills without endangering lives. Today the coaster's overwhelming popularity in amusement parks around the world is the result of ingenious design, engineering skill, and the application of psychology.

Imagine that Rick has completed the first part of his conclusion by reminding his audience of the major points made in support of his thesis statement. He hopes that by now the audience shares some of his enthusiasm.

For a strong finish, he might consider one of the following ideas:

- How the **names** of many coasters emphasize their goal of terrifying the rider: Millennium Force, Hell Fire, Cliff Hanger, Mind Eraser, Exterminator, Disaster Transport.

- The remarkable **evolution** of the roller coaster from the Gravity Switchback Railroads of 1884 to the tallest, fastest, most complex coasters of today's amusement parks.

- The **variety of features** in contemporary coaster design: inverted cars, corkscrews, free-falls, knife-edge turns, 180° barrel rolls, speed spirals, and loops (diving, vertical, oblique).

- How the popularity of coasters—13 new ones already under construction in 2009—might connect with the rise of **extreme sports**—sky surfing, mega-ramp skateboarding, ski-biking, BMX racing, base jumping, wave jumping, and the like.

- How the roller coaster has become a **symbol** of the quest for ever more intense thrills, and what this says about contemporary American life.

- The **future development** of coasters: what new, fantastic features will designers dream up to terrify the next generation?

- The role of **computer-assisted design** tools in the future: how might they add to the many varieties of coasters currently in use throughout the world?

- The matter of **safety**: although reliable statistics are hard to come by, some reports estimate that there are an average of three roller coaster-related fatalities in the United States each year, and many more injuries. Is riding a coaster really "safer than riding a bicycle"?

© 2009. Teacher's Discovery®

- The implications of an **apt quotation** such as the following: Charles Lindberg: "A ride on the Cyclone is a greater thrill than flying an airplane at top speed," or the familiar saying, "A carousel is the soul of an amusement park, but a roller coaster is its heart."

Based on these suggestions, practice writing the concluding paragraph for Rick's essay. Then think about how to apply these ideas to take a thesis statement beyond and bring it to a satisfying close. Can the history of roller coasters reveal anything about the psychology of pleasure? Can a prediction be formed regarding future development? Can a provocative question be raised? Is there an unresolved problem that can be pursued?

© 2009. Teacher's Discovery®

Step 8 Summary

To move from notes to rough draft:

- Sort the note cards into piles under each major heading and number them in the order they are to be used. Work one body section at a time.

- Support a topic sentence with information from the note cards, using paraphrase, summary, and direct quotation, and providing all needed citations.

- Use lead-ins to introduce direct quotations and follow-ups to provide discussion of all borrowed material.

- Print out each section, highlighting and numbering borrowed material in order to see where it may need additional ideas and comments.

- Read over each section, revising and improving, adding and deleting. Then go on to the next section. Save all materials—outlines, cards, printouts, copies, and drafts.

The introduction paragraph

- includes focusing sentences, thesis, and method of development.

- sets the tone, generates interest.

- includes refocusing sentences, reminder of thesis, and brief recapitulation.

The conclusion paragraph

- goes beyond the thesis statement by suggesting implications, raising questions, or enlarging the context.

- reflects the introduction.

© 2009. Teacher's Discovery®

Step 9

Revising and Proofreading

Polishing the Writing

Feedback from Others

Final Checklist for Revising and Proofreading

Proofreading and Correction Symbols

© 2009. Teacher's Discovery®

From the time the rough draft is started until the research paper is turned in, the process of revision continues. Although it is impossible to list all the ways that writing can be improved, this chapter offers suggestions and highlights areas of common weakness. Included is a checklist, guidelines for getting feedback from others, and a list of frequently used correction symbols to aid in understanding teacher and classmate suggestions (feedback). Since many schools and departments have their own rules, be sure to follow local guidelines. When in doubt, ask the teacher.

Another important aspect of revising and proofreading is learning from mistakes made. It's a good idea to keep a portfolio of work, where strengths and weaknesses can be noted as corrected assignments are returned. When a teacher or other students identify errors or writing weaknesses, work to avoid those problems in future assignments. It's also important to notice what has been done well in order to build on those strengths.

Polishing the Writing

The following items are stylistic choices that can weaken the delivery and presentation of an argument. Read through the paper carefully, looking for these writing weaknesses. Circle the weaknesses on the rough draft. With classmates/peer editors, work on alternative words or phrases that will strengthen the writing. Edit the final draft to show these necessary revisions.

Issues Requiring Revision

Issue 1. Overuse of passive voice can result in awkward passages. Circle all uses of passive verbs and compose alternative wording.

> ┌─**Example**────────────────────────────────────
> Passive voice: This book was written by Fitzgerald during the 1930s.
>
> Active voice: Fitzgerald wrote this book during the 1930s.

Issue 2. Formal academic writing standards dictate the use of formal English. Circle all slang words or phrases. Circle all informal phrases or constructions. Circle clichés. Provide alternative wording or syntax.

Issue 3. Avoid using empty words such as *very, really*, or *quite*. Circle these words and choose stronger adjectives that will negate the need for these qualifiers.

Issue 4. Circle all uses of overworked words and phrases such as *interesting, thing, due to the fact, involved with, obviously, importantly, actually,* etc. Most of them can be omitted or replaced with more meaningful transition words, such as *therefore, while,* or *because of*.

Issue 5. Vary sentence structure throughout the paper. Note areas of syntactical repetition. Compose alternative sentence constructions.

Issue 6. Observe any repetition of specific words or phrases that are not used for a specific stylistic effect. Choose variations in word choice and phrasing.

Issue 7. Circle all use of general reference pronouns such as *this, that,* and *it*. Include a clear antecedent or provide a definite noun to replace the unclear pronoun.

Issue 8. Transitions are important tools that guide the reader through the logic of the paper. Use them frequently to improve coherence of the paper.

© 2009. Teacher's Discovery®

Getting Feedback From Others

Many students are accustomed to exchanging papers with other students in order to get feedback; in fact, most teachers require peer editing in class before the final product is due. Whether or not it is required, having a pair of eyes other than the writer's review the paper reveals problems that would be otherwise missed. Of course, this peer editor can discover errors in punctuation and spelling, but an understanding of the thesis and the supporting work is important. If he or she cannot identify the main ideas as suggested in the paragraphs that follow, it indicates that the paper is not yet clear, logical, or coherent.

Have the external reviewer use these guidelines to edit the paper. A reproducible Feedback and Review Checklist following these guidelines can be found in Appendix A on pages 159-160.

Overview

Person   Has the author avoided use of first- and second-person pronouns: *I, me, you, we,* etc.? Circle all use of first- and second-person pronouns in the essay, except when in direct quotes.

Tense   Literature is always referred to in the present tense. Did the author use present-tense verbs when discussing situations in books or poems? Historical events are referred to in the past tense, and scientific research reports generally use past tense. Circle all instances where the author didn't follow these rules.

Quotes   When the author introduces quotes and displays the credentials of the cited person, did the author follow up with discussion using phrasing other than *this quote means/indicates …*? Circle all places where the author's use of this phrasing requires rephrasing.

Citations   Is citation completed correctly according to the required style guidelines? Circle all references that are improperly cited.

Grammar   Circle any grammatical or mechanical errors. Suggest an alternative approach that may correct the problem.

Weakness   Look for writing weaknesses, such as passive voice, vagueness, verbosity, redundancy, etc. Suggest alternatives.

Introductory Paragraph(s)

Opening Statement

Is there an opening statement that focuses the reader's attention and introduces the general subject? Underline and label the sentence(s) with a colored pen.

Thesis Statement

Find the thesis statement and underline and label it with a colored pen. Does the thesis announce the main purpose of the essay and does the thesis propose an interesting topic worthy of discussion?

Method of Development

Underline and label with a colored pen the method of development (MOD). Does the MOD cover at least two distinct topics that can be used to prove or further explain the thesis? Number these stated topics. Are these areas stated clearly? Does the MOD blend well with the rest of the introductory paragraph?

Additional Information

Record additional comments and/or questions about the introductory paragraph on a separate piece of paper.

© 2009. Teacher's Discovery®

Body Paragraphs

Clear MOD

Are there clear body sections covering the topics addressed in the MOD? Number these sections as they correspond to the MOD.

Topic Sentences

Does each body paragraph contain a topic sentence detailing the general idea to be discussed? Does each topic sentence make a clear connection between the content of the paragraph and the purpose of the paper as stated by the thesis? Underline and label the topic sentences with a colored pen.

Support From Sources

Does each body section contain paraphrases and direct quotes? Are they cited correctly? Does the author integrate these into the flow of the paper? Does the author use lead-ins and follow-ups?

Making the Connections

Does the author fully, comprehensively, and clearly explain the connection between the borrowed material and his/her thesis statement?

Additional Information

Record additional comments and/or questions about the body paragraphs on a separate piece of paper.

Conclusion Paragraph(s)

New Ideas

Does the conclusion paragraph present any new ideas that were not discussed in the body of the paper? If so, cross these ideas out or reassign them to their proper place in the body paragraphs.

Summarizing

Does the conclusion concisely sum up the ideas presented in the body of this paper?

MOD Restatement

Underline the restated MOD and label it with a colored pen.

Thesis Restatement

Does the conclusion restate the thesis using different words? Underline the restated thesis and label it with a colored pen.

Closure

Does the conclusion bring closure to the paper and satisfaction to the reader?

Additional Information

Record additional comments and/or questions about the body paragraphs on a separate piece of paper.

Holistic

1. **Give a detailed explanation of the degree of the paper's argument as strong, weak, or somewhere in the middle.**

2. **How does it flow?**

3. **Is the paper structurally sound?**

4. **Provide no fewer than three suggestions of how the author can improve the paper.**

© 2009. Teacher's Discovery®

Final Checklist for Revising and Proofreading

Formatting

The author has

✓   used standard, readable 12-point typeface and set margins at one inch on all sides.

✓   set a tab to indent one-half inch (or five spaces) to begin each paragraph.

✓   followed these formatting guides for the title:

- centered the title on the line of the first page.

- skipped a line after the title and before the first line of the essay.

- refrained from underlining the title or putting the title in quotation marks.

- capitalized only the first letter of the first word, the first letter of the last word, and the first letter of all the principal words (including nouns, pronouns, verbs, adjectives, adverbs, and subordinating conjunctions). Exceptions include articles (a, an, the) when they occur in the middle of the title, prepositions (no matter how many letters), coordinating conjunctions, and the word *to* in infinitives.

✓   double-spaced text, including long direct quotations and the works cited page or references page, throughout the paper.

✓   observed teacher instructions about the heading (the placement of name, subject, and date).

Mechanics, Usage, and Style

The author has

✓   made the writing style appropriate to the subject, assignment, and audience and avoided contractions, abbreviations, colloquialisms, and slang.

✓   run a spelling and grammar check after each addition to or revision of the paper and corrected misspellings, typos, and other errors; personally proofread the paper and had at least one additional human being proofread it.

✓   checked the entire paper for the following:

- errors in grammar and usage.

- consistency in point of view and verb use—maintaining one tense throughout the essay except where a tense shift is appropriate.

- use of present tense in discussion of literature and literary criticism.

- use of third person in literary analysis and expository writing except where a shift to first person is appropriate.

- errors in punctuation, with particular attention to the period after the parenthetical citation, except in the case of long, indented quotations.

✓   italicized all titles of books, plays, long poems, periodicals, films, musicals, radio and television programs, compact discs, audiocassettes, works of art, and reference works, both within the text and the documentation of the paper.

© 2009. Teacher's Discovery®

✓ placed quotation marks around the titles of stories, poems, essays, songs, chapters, and the like.

✓ observed all instructions about formatting, pagination, heading, cover sheet, etc., whether writing at home or at school.

✓ read the entire rough draft aloud at least once, in order to catch awkwardness, repetition, and faulty logic. The ear will catch much that the eye misses.

✓ consulted an authority whenever in doubt.

Documentation and Use of Borrowed Material

The author has

✓ used a variety of sources without relying heavily on one over the others, used print sources as well as Internet sources, and checked the Internet sources for reliability.

✓ used no borrowed material in the paper that is not on the note cards and can produce all sources on demand; has avoided plagiarism through thorough paraphrasing and accurate documentation, both for in-text citations and on the works cited or references page.

✓ checked all borrowed material for proper use and accuracy and correctly used summarizing, thorough paraphrasing, or direct quotations, enclosing direct quotations in quotation marks and showing omissions with ellipses.

✓ provided sources for all borrowed material, whether directly or indirectly quoted, paraphrased, or summarized, and given parenthetical citations in the correct format.

✓ developed and expanded upon the borrowed material so that the paper does not merely state facts but explains, comments, and provides connections; integrated quotes into the discussion instead of just stringing them together, and included personal ideas and analysis.

✓ checked the works cited or references page, making sure that the entries do the following:

- include **all** the works mentioned in the paper.

- include **only** the works mentioned in the paper.

- are alphabetized, not numbered.

- are punctuated and capitalized according to MLA or APA rules.

- correspond to the sources cited within the paper's text.

Structure and Content

The author has

✓ ensured that the thesis paragraph contains focusing sentences, thesis statement, and method of development; the body paragraphs have strong topic sentences and present material that supports the thesis statement.

✓ used transitions throughout the paper, creating smooth shifts from one idea to the next.

✓ paid strict attention to addressing all corrections, comments, and questions that have come from teachers and/or classmates, in an effort to continue to improve the paper in the ways that have been suggested.

✓ worked to make sure this paper reflects superior personal efforts.

© 2009. Teacher's Discovery®

Proofreading and Correction Symbols

A reproducible version of this checklist can be found on page 161.

Individual teachers, schools, style manuals, and dictionaries all suggest different ways to indicate errors in written work. The notation given here includes symbols that many teachers and students find useful as shorthand to mark errors and suggest improvements. Examples follow the error or writing weakness when appropriate. A short version of these lists is available on pages 157-158.

Usages	Symbol	Example
Spelling error	*sp*	We woud like more broccoli. [would]
Close up space; print as one word	⌒	Every body; basket ball.
Delete, or word crossed out; take it out	ℓ	The squirrels up in our attic are an annoying nuisance.
Insert missing word or needed punctuation	∧	The troll at the bridge would not let pass. *the goats*
Insert space	#	After school, we headed for Great Falls.
Transpose elements; change the order	∿	recieve; After a many sleepless night
Punctuation error(s)	*ρ* and ∧	Men women and children ran in all directions. The twins were chanting Ants! Ants! Ants wear underpants.
Use a lowercase letter	*ℓc* and /	I plan to study Sociology and Basket Weaving in College.
Capitalization error(s); use a capital letter	*c, cap,* and ≡	In english I'm reading a novel about indians.
Begin a new paragraph; indent	¶	… Vonnegut's novel *Slaughterhouse-Five* has been banned time after time. ¶Bruce Severy, a teacher at Drake High School in North Dakota who taught *Slaughterhouse-Five*, defended it …
Do not begin a new paragraph	*no* ¶	… Vonnegut's novel *Slaughterhouse-Five* has been banned time after time. *no* ¶ Bruce Severy, a teacher at Drake High School in North Dakota who taught *Slaughterhouse-Five*, defended it …

© 2009. Teacher's Discovery®

Symbol	Usages
shift/t	Shift from one tense to another—e.g., past to present.
shift/pov	Shift from one point of view to another—e.g., first person to third. Be consistent in the use of verb tenses and point of view.
?	Vague or ambiguous; make the meaning clear.
awk	Awkward, clumsy phrasing or sentence structure; rewrite sentence, striving for grace, balance, and clarity.
trans	Transition needed; provide transitional words or phrases to link ideas, sentences, and paragraphs.
coh	Problems with coherence; paragraph lacks unity and organization; does not hang together. Rethink the focus; re-examine the thesis statement (Th S), topic sentence (TS), and supporting ideas.

Faulty sentence structure; specific errors may include the following:

Usages	Symbol	Example
Sentence fragment or incomplete sentence; add the missing parts, often the main verb	*frag*	Because our teamwork was superior. Under the stairway, where no one had looked.
Run-on sentence, also called comma splice; two sentences run together with no punctuation or joined only by a comma; provide the correct punctuation	*r-o*	We're planning a party, we've invited everyone. Jane wrote the lyrics, Carlos composed the music.
Dangling or misplaced modifier; rearrange the sentence	*dm* *mm*	Racing toward the finish, a pothole made him stumble. Samantha saw a dog gnawing a bone on her way to school.

© 2009. Teacher's Discovery®

Usages	Symbol	Example
Faulty parallel structure; when presenting a series, be consistent in the use of specific parts of speech, infinitives, and verbs	//	We held a bake sale, a car wash, and we sold raffle tickets. The club president's duties include planning the program, running the meetings, and to make sure that new members feel welcome.
Passive voice; make the verbs active; give the grammatical subject of the sentence the action	pv	Active: The aardvark ate my birthday cake. Passive: My birthday cake was eaten by the aardvark.
Lack of agreement between subject and verb (s-v) or between pronoun and antecedent (p-a); make both singular or both plural	agr	Neither Matthew nor Hannah know the answer. Everyone should open their books to page 17.
Wrong word; word does not have the meaning suggested	ww	He flaunted the rules until the principal expelled him. [The writer means *flout*, not *flaunt*].
Weak word choice; tone or level of language inappropriate	wc	A bunch of guys started harassing us kids; the thing about it was, the fight became pretty interesting.
Grammatical error	gr	Between you and I, she is a liar and a thief. When I saw him laying on the floor, I almost died.
Faulty logic	log	It's not true that smoking causes cancer; my grandfather smokes a pack a day and he's 85. The astronauts saw no angels in outer space, so obviously angels don't exist.
Wordiness	w	The alarm, which I set the night before, went off extremely early at 6 a.m. before the sun came up at dawn.
Needless repetition	rep	In Salinger's novel, Salinger shows many of the problems of adolescents and young people.
Redundancy	red	salty brine; hot water heater; pizza pie
Indefinite reference	ir or ref	As the creature emerged from the black lagoon, it was silent. [The reference of it is unclear].

© 2009. Teacher's Discovery®

Step 9 Summary

To revise and proofread a paper, take a close look at

- formatting, including type, margins, indentation, spacing, title, and heading.

- mechanics, including grammar, spelling, capitalization, and punctuation.

- style and usage, including word choice, sentence variety and length, and appropriateness of language to specific task.

- structure, including introduction with focusing sentences, thesis statement, and method of development. Body paragraphs should have clear topic sentences and transitions throughout.

- conclusion with restated thesis, recapitulation, and sentences that go *beyond*.

- use of borrowed material, including paraphrasing, summarizing, and direct quotation.

- lead-ins and follow-ups for direct quotations; variety of sources.

- documentation, including accurate parenthetical citations, works cited or references.

© 2009. Teacher's Discovery®

Step 10

Preparing the Citation Page

MLA: The Works Cited Page

MLA: Examples of Works Cited Entries

APA: The References Page

APA: Examples of Reference List Entries

© 2009. Teacher's Discovery®

This final step provides the rules and examples that are needed to prepare the works cited page for a research paper, the last step in a long journey. Providing full information about the sources is an essential aspect of being a responsible researcher. Since the MLA and the APA give quite different specifications, a separate section for each format is provided. **Be sure to use the format that is required.**

Many services such as NoodleBib, EasyBib, or Son of Citation Machine prepare the works cited page based on the source card entries. However, as discussed previously, these services are not always up-to-date and require that the correct resource type is selected and that all of the relevant data is entered. When using one of these programs, double check the final product to ensure it is in accordance with the most recent style guidelines.

To prepare the works cited page without an aid, begin by putting aside any cards for sources that have not been used. Then check the remaining source cards for any errors or omissions. **Remember, all ideas and information that are borrowed must be cited, and the works cited listings must match the parenthetical citations within the text of the paper.**

MLA: The Works Cited Page

Task 1. Arrange cards alphabetically by author.

Do not number the entries on the works cited page. Check the model.

Where there is no author, as in unsigned newspaper, magazine, or other articles, use the title of the article, alphabetizing according to the first significant word in the title.

Task 2. Punctuate carefully.

Italicize book titles, plays, long poems, pamphlets, periodicals (newspapers, magazines, journals), films, radio and television programs, compact discs, ballets, operas, and other long musical compositions, paintings, and works of sculpture.

Put quotation marks around the titles of articles, essays, chapters, poems, short stories, and episodes of radio and television programs. The entries should match the models provided here.

Task 3. Double check publication information

┌─ **Example** ──────────────────────────────
Remember to shorten publishers' names:

W.W. Norton — Norton

Harcourt Brace — Harcourt

Simon and Schuster — Simon

Charles Scribner's Sons — Scribner's

Princeton University Press — Princeton UP

Holt, Rinehart and Winston — Holt
└──

When in doubt, check section 7.5 in the *MLA Handbook*, or ask the teacher.

Task 4. Capitalize the first letter of all words except articles (a, an, the) when they occur in the middle of the title, prepositions, coordinating conjunctions (and, or, nor, for, yet, so, but), and *to* in infinitives.

> **┌Example ───**
>
> *A Tale of Two Cities*
>
> *Black Voices: An Anthology of Afro-American Literature*
>
> "Ode to a Nightingale" [poem]
>
> "Fitzgerald: The Horror and the Vision of Paradise" [short story]
>
> "The Worms of the Earth against the Lions" [chapter]

Task 5. Start a separate digital file for the works cited page

- Begin the works cited at the top of a new page.
- The title Works Cited—no quotation marks, no underline, with proper title capitalization—is placed at the center on the top line of the page.
- Double-space the entire works cited page.
- Begin each entry flush with the left margin.
- Indent five spaces (or one-half inch) all lines following the first for each entry.
- Use ---. instead of repeating an author's name for the second entry by the same writer.
- Proofread carefully.
- Number the works cited page consecutively with the rest of the paper. If the paper ends on page 7, then the works cited page is page 8.
- For the form of any entries not included on this page, check the examples that follow.

An example of a works cited page (from Paloma's paper on film and musical versions of *Adventures of Huckleberry Finn*) follows on the next page. All works cited pages use this same format regardless of a paper's subject matter.

Example

Works Cited

Bollinger, Laurel. "Say It, Jim: The Morality of Connection in *Adventures of Huckleberry Finn*."

College Literature 29 (2002): 32-53. *Literature Resource Center*. Web. 8 March 2007.

Cope, Virginia H., ed. *Mark Twain's Huckleberry Finn: Text, Illustrations, and Early Reviews*.

Electronic Text Center. U of Virginia, 1995. Web. 8 March 2007

Haupt, Clyde V. *Huckleberry Finn on Film: Film and Television Adaptations of Mark Twain's*

Novel, 1920-1993. Jefferson: McFarland, 1994. Print.

Hearn, Michael Patrick, ed. *The Annotated Huckleberry Finn: Huckleberry Finn (Tom Sawyer's*

Comrade). By Mark Twain [Samuel L. Clemens]. 1885. New York: Norton, 2001. Print.

Hill, Dick, narr. *Adventures of Huckleberry Finn: The Classic Collection*. By Mark Twain.

Brilliance Audio, 2001. CD.

Miller, Roger. *Big River*. Perf. Rene Auberjonois, Patti Cohenour, John Goodman, Bob Gunton,

Susan Browning, Gordon Connell. Rec. 1985. Decca, 1990. DVD.

Murray, Matthew. Rev. of *Big River: The Adventures of Huckleberry Finn*.

Talkinbroadway.com. TalkinBroadway Inc., 24 July 2003. Web. 8 March 2007.

Rich, Frank. "With Huck Finn on *Big River*." *New York Times*. New York Times, 26 April 1985.

Web. 8 March 2007.

MLA: Examples of Works Cited Entries

Books

Book by One Author

Pinker, Steven. *The Language Instinct: How the Mind Creates Language*. New York: Harper, 2007. Print.

Two or More Books by the Same Author

Friedman, Thomas L. *Hot, Flat, and Crowded: Why We Need A Green Revolution—And How It Can Renew America*. New York: Farrar, 2008. Print.

---*The World Is Flat: A Brief History of the Twenty-First Century*. New York: Farrar, 2007. Print.

Book by Two Authors

Frum, David, and Richard Perle. *An End to Evil: How to Win the War on Terror*. New York: Random, 2004. Print.

Book by Three (or more) Authors

Coaffee, Jon, David Murakami Wood, and Peter Rogers. *The Everyday Resilience of the City: How Cities Respond to Terrorism and Disaster*. New York: Palgrave-Macmillan, 2009. Print.

Book by a Corporate Author

Office for Intellectual Freedom. *Intellectual Freedom Manual*. 7th ed. Chicago: American Library Association, 2005. Print.

Work in an Anthology or Compilation (essay, speech, poem, or short story)

Truth, Sojourner. "Ar'n't I a Woman." *Norton Anthology of African American Literature*. Ed. Henry Louis Gates Jr. and Nellie Y. McKay. 2nd ed. New York: Norton, 2003. 196-198. Print.

Tanner, Tony. "Afterthoughts on Don DeLillo's *Underworld*." Rev. of *Underworld*, by Don DeLillo. Raritan 17 (1998): 48-71. Rpt. in *Contemporary Literary Criticism*. Vol. 143. Detroit: Gale, 2001. 206-15. Print.

Williams, Carol T. "Nabokov's Dozen Short Stories: His World in Microcosm." *Studies in Short Fiction* 12 (1975): 213-22. Rpt. in *Twentieth Century American Literature*. Ed. Harold Bloom. Vol. 5. New York: Chelsea, 1987. 2807-11. Print.

Book with an Editor as Author

Wetmore, Kevin J., ed. *Revenge Drama in European Renaissance and Japanese Theater: From Hamlet to Madame Butterfly*. New York: Macmillan, 2008. Print.

Article in a Specialized Reference Work

"Anna Klumpke." *Encyclopedia of Lesbian, Gay, Bisexual and Transgendered History in America.* Ed. Mark Stein. New York: Scribner's, 2003. Print.

Unsigned Article in an Encyclopedia

"Chaos Theory." *Columbia Encyclopedia.* 6th ed. 2001. Print.

"Existentialism." *Encyclopedia Britannica.* 2007 ed. Print.

Introduction, Preface, Foreword, or Afterword

Emerson, Steven. Foreward. *Defeating Political Islam: The New Cold War.* By Moorthy S. Muthuswamy. Amherst: Promethius, 2009. Print.

Anonymous Book

New York Public Library Desk Reference. 4th ed. New York: Hyperion, 2002. Print.

Holy Bible. Authorized King James Version. London: Collins, 1949. Print.

Translation

Chaucer, Geoffrey. *The Canterbury Tales.* Trans. Burton Raffel. New York: Modern Library-Random, 2008. Print.

Pamphlet

Committee on Patient Education of the American College of Obstetricians and Gynecologists. *Women's Health: Depression.* Washington DC: American College of Obstetricians and Gynecologists, 2008. Print.

Government Publication

Long Passage to Korea: Black Sailors and the Integration of the United States Navy. Washington: GPO, 2003. Print.

Multivolume Work (if more than one volume is used)

Sadie, Stanley, and John Tyrrell, eds. *The New Grove Dictionary of Music and Musicians.* 2nd ed. 29 vols. London: Macmillan, 2001. Print.

A Multivolume Work (if only one volume is used)

Sadie, Stanley, and John Tyrrell, eds. *The New Grove Dictionary of Music and Musicians.* 2nd ed. Vol. 5. London: Macmillan, 2001. Print.

© 2009. Teacher's Discovery®

Periodicals

Article in a Scholarly Journal

Ganem, Don, and Alfred M. Prince. "Hepatitis B Virus Infection—Natural History and Consequences." *New England Journal of Medicine* 350 (2004): 1118-29. Print.

Grcic, Joseph. "Truth in Ethics: A Pragmatic Approach." *Prima-Philosophia* 16.1 (2003): 43-59. Print.

Article in a Magazine

Nordhaus, Ted and Michael Shellenberger. "The Green Bubble: Why Environmentalism Keeps Imploding." *The New Republic* 20 May 2009: 16-18. Print.

Unsigned Magazine Article

"The Washington Dauphin." *The Weekly Standard* 18 May 2009: 2. Print.

Document

Truman, Harry S. "The Recall of General Douglas MacArthur." *Documents of American History since 1898*. Ed. Henry Steele Commager. Englewood Cliffs: Prentice, 1973: 67-69. Print.

Article in a Newspaper

Whitlock, Craig. "Spain's Judges Cross Borders in Rights Cases." *Washington Post* 24 May 2009: A1+. Print.

Burns, John F. "The Road Ahead May Be Even Rougher." *New York Times* 7 Mar. 2004, New England ed., sec. 4:1. Print.

Editorial in a Newspaper

"California Sinking: The Case Against a Federal Bailout." Editorial. *Washington Post* 24 May 2009: A20. Print.

Letter to the Editor

Davar, Tamina. Letter. Christian *Science Monitor* 9 Mar. 2004: 8. Print.

Review

Olszewski, Tricia. "All Things Sequel." Rev. of *Night at the Museum: Battle of the Smithsonian,* dir. Shawn Levy. *Washington City Paper* 22-28 May 2009: 38. Print.

Miller, Laura. "Faking It." Rev. of *Lost in the Meritocracy: The Undereducation of an Overachiever,* by Walter Kirn. *New York Review of Books* 24 May 2009: 7. Print.

Other Sources

To cite these sources in their original forms, use the models here. For examples showing how to cite these items when they are found online, refer to the section on citing a work on the Web with publication data for non-print media.

Television or Radio Program

"Ocean Animal Emergency." *Nova.* PBS. WETA, Washington, D.C. 26 May 2009. Television.

Sound Recording

Bruckner, Anton. *Symphony No. 5 in B Minor.* Perf. London Philharmonic Orchestra. Rec. 8-10 Jan. 2008. Telarc, 2009. CD.

Muhaiyaddeen, M. R. Bawa. *Islam and World Peace: Explanations of a Sufi.* Read by M.E. Willis. Audio Literature, 2002. CD.

Film, Filmstrip, Slide Program, or Video Recording

Chaplin, Charles, dir. *City Lights.* Perf. Chaplin and Virginia Cherrill. 1931. Chaplin Collection, vol. 2. Warner, 2004. DVD.

Performance

Twelfth Night. By William Shakespeare. Dir. Josie Rourke. Perf. Karen Aldridge and Michelle Beck. Chicago Shakespeare Company. Carl and Marilynn Thoma Theater, Chicago. 10 Apr. 2009. Performance.

Published Musical Composition

Joplin, Scott. *Treemonisha.* Vocal Score. New York: Dover, 2001. Print.

Work of Art

Brueghel, Pieter. *Landscape with the Fall of Icarus.* Oil on Canvas. Musées Royaux des Beaux-Arts, Brussels.

Letter

Ondaatje, Michael. Letter to the author. 14 Jan. 2003.

Fitzgerald, Zelda. "To F. Scott Fitzgerald." 12 April 1934. *Correspondence of F. Scott Fitzgerald.* Eds. Matthew J. Bruccoli and Margaret Duggan. New York: Random, 1980.351-352. Print.

Interview

Jackson, Jesse. Telephone interview. 5 Jan. 2009.

Luntz, Frank. "Questions for Frank Luntz, the Wordsmith." By Deborah Solomon. *New York Times* 24 May 2009, New York ed.: MM 17. Print.

© 2009. Teacher's Discovery®

Map or Chart

Vermont. Map. Montpelier: Vermont Attractions Assoc., 2003.

Lecture, Speech, Address

Obama, Barack. *State of the Union.* United States Congress, Washington D.C. 24 Feb. 2009. Speech.

Cartoon

Toles, Tom. Editorial Cartoon. *The Washington Post 3* June 2009: A18. Print.

E-Mail

Perkins, Seth. "Re: Your campaign for the presidency." E-mail to Ralph Nader. 15 Mar. 2004.

Walsh, Samantha. E-mail to the author. 18 Jan. 2008.

Electronic Sources

Although the rules for documenting electronic sources have undergone a number of changes since the advent of the Internet, the MLA has established clear rules for these references. As with print citations, author, document title, information about publication, and medium are all required. In addition, because electronic sources are not as stable as their print counterparts, these citations also require title of the database or webpage as well as the date of access.

Because electronic sources are so varied and because some electronic sources do not include full bibliographic information, the MLA advises researchers to record whatever information is available, in a format that is internally consistent. It also cautions that researchers may need to be prepared to improvise in order to record information in complex publications, and that the print citation recommendations will often provide useful guidelines in dealing with aspects not directly addressed by the MLA Handbook.

Where complete information is not available, provide as much information as can be found.

The most recent version of the MLA Handbook gives the researcher discretionary judgment over whether to include the URL (uniform resource locator) in a citation. Generally, these do not need to be included, but, if the researcher determines that a reader would probably not be able to find the source without the URL, then the researcher should include it. Likewise, some teachers will require the inclusion of the URL. In these cases, the URL belongs immediately after the date of access. It should be enclosed in angle brackets (<>) and followed by a period after the closing bracket. Divide a URL only after a slash (/).

Example

Benson, L. D. "Courtly Love" *The Geoffrey Chaucer Page.* Harvard University, 5 July 2006. Web. 25 May 2009. <http://www.courses.fas.harvard.edu/~chaucer/ special/lifemann/love/>.

© 2009. Teacher's Discovery®

Work Cited Only on the Web

Most web documents, whether they are a home page, a page within a larger website collection, a sound recording, or an image, will be cited using these guidelines, since the majority of web documents are not considered to be periodical, meaning that they are not published on a regular basis. Generally included in this category are magazines and newspapers (that are not found using an electronic database). These guidelines are for documents found on the Web that do not include data about a source that may have appeared in another medium. The sections on citing web documents that appeared in another medium, such as a film that was digitized for viewing in a browser or a book that was scanned to the webpage, are found following this section.

Include the following information:

1. Name of the author, compiler, director, editor, narrator, or translator. Follow print guidelines for more than one author, for a corporate author, or for an anonymous work.

2. Title of the work. (In quotation marks if it is part of a larger work; italicized if it is independent)

3. Title of the overall website (italicized), if not the same as the title of the work.

4. Version or edition used, if available.

5. Publisher or sponsor of the site. If not available, use N.p.

6. Date of publication (day, month, and year). If no date is available, use n.d.

7. Medium of publication (Web).

8. Date of access (day, month, year).

Webpages

Ockerbloom, John Mark, ed. "Banned Books Online." *Online Books Page*, U of Penn. 22 May 2009. Web. 25 May 2009.

Hamilton, Mary H. "Ezra Jack Keats: Biography." *De Grummond Children's Literature Research Collection*, U of Southern Mississippi. 26 April 2002. Web. 25 May 2009.

Map

"New Mexico." Map. *Google Maps*. Google, 20 April 2008. Web. 20 April 2008.

Sound Recording

Baker, Peter, narr. "Beowulf's Funeral." *Old English Homepage*. University of Virginia English Department, n.d. Web. 3 Feb. 2009.

Newspaper Article Found Online (Not From a Database)

Fish, Stanley. "Empathy and the Law." Editorial. *New York Times*. New York Times, 24 May 2009. Web. 24 May 2009.

"Anger Over North Korea Nuclear Test." *BBC News, International Version*. British Broadcasting Corporation, 25 May 2009. Web. 28 May 2009.

© 2009. Teacher's Discovery®

Online Encyclopedia

"Aphrodite." *Encyclopædia Britannica Online*. Encyclopædia Britannica, 2009. Web. 2 Mar. 2009.

Magazine Article Found Online (Not From a Database)

Sayle, Carol Ann. "The Downside of Year-Round Farming." *The Atlantic.com*. Atlantic Monthly Group, 25 May 2009. Web. 1 June 2009.

Online Scholarly Journal

This format should only be used with scholarly journals that are published independently on the Web. Articles from scholarly journals that are accessed via an online database should use the appropriate form for information procured by a database. To cite a work in a scholarly journal found only on the Web, follow the guidelines for a print periodical, but replace the print designation with Web and include the date of access If the work does not include page numbers, use n.pag. to denote this.

Krstic, Igor. "Rethinking Serbia: A Psychoanalytic Reading of Modern Serbian History and Identity through Popular Culture." *Other Voices: The (e)Journal of Cultural Criticism* 2.2 (2002): n.pag. Web. 21 Mar. 2004.

Hershock, Peter D. "From Vulnerability to Virtuosity: Buddhist Reflections on Responding to Terrorism and Tragedy." *Journal of Buddhist Ethics* 10 (2003): n.pag. Web. 14 Jan. 2007.

Work on the Web Cited with Print Publication Data

To cite an article, poem, short story, or other document that is found on the Web but that also appears in print, follow the guidelines for print publication citations (i.e., anthology, translation, multivolume work, etc.), but remove the "print" designation as the medium of publication. Instead, include the following: title of the database or website (italicized), medium of publication (Web), and date of access.

Examples

Douglass, Frederick. "Reconstruction." *Atlantic Monthly* 1866: 71-75. *Electronic Text Center*. U of Virginia Library, Feb. 1994. Web. 31 Jan. 2008.

Dickinson, Emily. "I like to see it lap the miles." *Complete Poems of Emily Dickinson*. Ed. Steven van Leeuwen. Boston: Little, 1924. N. pag. *Great Books Online*. Bartelby.com, 2000. Web. 20 Mar. 2004.

Montgomery, L.M. *Anne of Green Gables. Project Gutenberg*, 27 June 2008. Web. 1 Dec. 2008.

"Among the Chinese on the Pacific Coast." *Harper's Weekly* 37 (1893): n.pag. *The Chinese in California*, 1850-1925. *American Memory Project*. Library of Congress, 28 Mar. 03. Web. 23 May 2009.

Work on the Web with Publication Data for Non-Print Media

The Web offers researchers access to photographs, films, sound recordings and other non-print resources. When a work on the Web is available in another medium—for example, a digitized version of a film or a scanned photograph—use the format for the non-print sources but omit the designation of the original medium and add the following: title of the database or website (italicized); medium of publication (Web); and date of access (day, month, and year).

Painting, Sculpture, or Photograph

Cezanne, Paul. *At the Water's Edge.* 1890. Oil on canvas. National Gallery of Art, Washington D.C. *The Collection.* Web. 8 May 2009.

Fuseli, Henry. *Lady Macbeth.* 1784. Oil on canvas. Louvre, Paris. *WebMuseum.* 14 July 2008.

Radio or Television Program

"Extra! Special! Roosevelt Inaugurated." Universal Studios. 1933. *Internet Archive.* Web. 15 Apr. 2009.

"Meltdown at Three Mile Island." *American Experience.* 5 Apr. 2004. *PBS Online.* Web. 10 Apr. 2007.

Film or Film Clip

Blackmun, Harry A. *Video Tape 1, Session 1, of The Harry A. Blackmun Oral History Project.* 6 July 1994. Lib. of Congress Research Centers. Web. 9 Mar. 2004.

Sound Recording or Sound Clip

"Arkansas Traveler." *Fiddle Tunes of the Old Frontier: The Henry Reed Collection.* Perf. Henry Reed. Rec. Alan Jabour, 28 Oct. 1967. *American Memory Project.* Lib. of Congress. Web. 3 Mar. 2008.

Cohen, Ed, Elizabeth Richmond-Garza, and John Paul Requelme. "Portraits of Oscar Wilde." *What's the Word?* 18 July 2003. *Modern Language Association.* Web. Mar. 15 2004.

Work in an Online Database

Online databases include many different types of materials, including proprietary content created by the company itself, reprinted articles, scanned works, and multimedia enhancements, to name a few. Often, databases significantly change the presentation and pagination of an item. Use the page designation assigned by the database. If no pagination is available, use n.pag. To cite these sources, in general, use the appropriate print or non-print citation format but remove the original medium of publication, and add the following: title of the database (italicized); medium of publication (Web); and date of access (day, month, year).

Examples

Gornek, Vivian. "Hiding in Plain Sight." *Women's Review of Books* 20.2 (Nov. 2007): 6. *Student Resource Center Gold.* Web. 26 May 2009.

"Barbary Pirates." *World History: The Modern Era* (2009): n. pag. *ABC-CLIO.* Web. 26 May 2009.

"Trying to Get Their Own Back: Iraq's Kurds." *Economist* 31 Jan. 2004: 53. *Proquest.* Web. 19 March 2007.

CD-ROM or DVD-ROM Programs

For non-periodical publications, include the following information: author's name or name of editor, compiler, or translator; title (italicized); edition or version; place of publication; publisher; date; medium of publication.

When citing only part of the work, state which part. If the part is a book-length work, then italicize the title. If the part is a shorter work, such as an article, essay, poem, or short story, enclose the title in quotation marks.

For periodical publications, include the author's name, original publication information, medium of publication consulted, title of the database (italicized), vendor's name, and publication date of the database.

Nonperiodical Publication on CD or DVD-ROM

Abrams, Harry R. *The Mystery of Magritte.* Brussels: Virtuo, 1997. CD-ROM.

"Pandora." *Oxford English Dictionary.* 2nd ed. Vers. 4.0. Oxford: Oxford UP, 2007. CD-ROM.

Periodically Published Database on CD or DVD-ROM

Roberts, Leslie. "Acid Rain: Forgotten, Not Gone." *U.S. News and World Report* 1 Nov. 1999: 70. *SIRS Researcher Mandarin.* ProQuest, 2001. CD-ROM.

The Rubayyat of Omar Khayyam. Internet Sacred Text Archive. Trans. Edward Fitzgerald. Ed. J. B. Hare. Vers. 8.0. Evinity, 2008. DVD-ROM.

APA: The Reference Page

Because the APA *Manual* is designed for professional researchers as well as for students, it includes many details and distinctions that go beyond what most high school students need. We have therefore omitted these details and present here only a shortened version of the APA rules. Most libraries, including school media centers, have a copy of the Publication *Manual of the American Psychological Association* (6th ed.). Consult it if necessary.

Despite some refinements over the years, the APA has established specific rules for citing online sources. Electronic sources follow the rules for their print counterparts, with the addition of the digital object identifier (DOI). This number can be found on the first page of the article, near the copyright notice, or in the document details or indexing function. If the article does not have a DOI number, cite the home page URL of the publication or database. If the article or webpage would be difficult to find from the home page, include the full URL address.

To follow APA guidelines, list on a page headed References the works cited within the research paper.

Task 1. Arrange cards alphabetically by author.

Where there is no author, as in unsigned newspaper, magazine, or other articles, use the title of the article and alphabetize according to the first significant word in the title. Alphabetize group authors by the first significant word of the name, as in American Psychological Association.

Task 2. Punctuate carefully.

- Abbreviations, such as chap., Rev. ed., p. (pp.), and vols., are acceptable.

- Italicize titles of the following: periodicals (e.g., journals, magazines, newspapers, newsletters, etc.), books, reports, brochures, monographs, manuals, and audiovisual media.

- Do not use quotation marks around chapters in books or titles of articles in journals, books, or magazines. The entries should match the models provided in this chapter.

- Double check the publication information. Provide full names for publishers:

> **Example**
>
> Harcourt Brace
>
> Prentice-Hall
>
> Pergamon Press
>
> Harvard University Press

Task 3. Capitalize titles according to these rules:

- For an article, chapter, or book, capitalize the first word only of title and subtitle, and any proper names.

- For the name of a magazine or newspaper, capitalize all words except articles (a, an, the), prepositions (in, on, of, between, among, etc.), and coordinating conjunctions (and, but, or, nor, so, for, yet). But capitalize the article if it is the first word of the title, as in *The Editorial Eye*.

© 2009. Teacher's Discovery®

Examples

Codd, R. T., & Cohen, B. N. (2003). Predicting college student intention to seek help for alcohol abuse. *Journal of Social and Clinical Psychology, 22*, 168-191.

Bersoff, D. N. (2003). *Ethical conflicts in psychology* (3rd ed.). Washington, DC: American Psychological Association.

Weiner, I. B. (Ed.). (2003). *Handbook of psychology* (Vols. 1-12). Hoboken, NJ: Wiley.

Strubbe, J. H., & Woods, S. C. (2004). The timing of meals. *Psychological Review, 111*, 128-141.

Task 4. Start a new file for the reference list, and start at the top of the page.

- Put the word References—without quotation marks or underlining, and not in all CAPS—at the center of the top line of the page.

- Double-space the entire references page.

- Start each entry at the left margin. Indent subsequent lines five spaces.

- List several works by the same author chronologically. Repeat the author's name.

- Proofread carefully.

- Number the references page consecutively with the rest of the paper. If the paper ends on page 7, then the references page is page 8.

- For the form of any entries not included under Task 3, check the examples that follow.

An example of a reference page illustrating the APA format follows on the next page.

Example

References

Brown, L. M., Shiang, J., & Bongar, B. (2003). Crisis intervention. In I. B. Weiner (Series Ed.),

    & G. Stricker & T. A. Wideger (Vol. Eds.), *Handbook of psychology*: Vol. 8. *Clinical*

    psychology (pp. 431- 451). Hoboken, NJ: Wiley.

Lazear, E. P. (2004). The Peter principle: A theory of decline. *Journal of Political Economy, 112*

    (Suppl.1), S141-163.

Montrose, V. T., Harris, W. E., & Moore, P. J. (2004). Sexual conflict and cooperation under

    naturally occurring male enforced monogamy. *Journal of Evolutionary Biology, 17*, 443-

    452.

Pervin, L. A., & John, O. (Eds.) (1999). *Handbook of personality: Theory and research.* (2nd

    ed.). New York: Guilford Press.

Rayler, N., & Oei, T. P. (2004). Role of culture in gambling and problem gambling. *Clinical*

    Psychology Review, 23, 1087-1114.

Rieger, G. Gygar, L., Linsenmeier, J., Siler-Knogl, A., Moskowitz, D., & Bailey, J.M. (2009).

    Sex typicality and attractiveness in childhood and adulthood: Assessing their

    relationships from videos. *Archives of Sexual Behavior*, n.p. doi: 10.1007/s10508-

    0099512-8

Shamdasani, S. (2003). *Jung and the making of modern psychology: The dream of science.*

    Cambridge, England: Cambridge University Press.

Swan, S., & Andrews, B. (2003). The relationship between shame, eating disorders and

    disclosure in treatment. *British Journal of Clinical Psychology, 42*, 367-378.

Tversky, A., & Gilovich, T. (2004). The cold facts about the "Hot Hand" in basketball. In Shafir,

    E. (Ed.), *Preference, belief, and similarity* (pp. 257-265). Cambridge: MIT Press.

    (Reprinted from *Chance, 2*, 1989, pp.16-21).

© 2009. Teacher's Discovery®

APA: Examples of Reference List Entries

Periodicals

Journal article, one author

Kruesi, L. (2009). Astronomers capture meager spiral. *Astronomy, 37(6)*, 16.

Journal article, two authors

Steltzer, H., & Post, E. (2009). Seasons and life cycles. *Science,* 324, 886-887.

Journal article, three to six authors

Antonuccio, D. O., Danton, W. G., & McClanahan, T. M. (2003). Psychology in the prescription era: Building a firewall between marketing and science. *American Psychologist,* 5, 1028-1043.

Journal article, more than six authors

Wittenbaum, G. M., Hollingshead, A. B., Paulus, P. B., Hirokawa, R. Y., Ancona, D. C., Peterson, R. S., … Yoon, K. (2004). The functional perspective as a lens for understanding groups. *Small Group Research,* 35(1), 17-43.

Online Journal Article, with DOI (digital object identifier)

Ward., T., & Salmon, K. (2009). The ethics of punishment: Correctional practice implications. *Aggression and Violent Behavior, 14(4)*, 239-247. doi: 10.1016/j.avb.2009.03.009

Online Journal Article, without DOI

Crystal, J. D., & Foote, A. L. (2009). Metacognition in animals. *Comparative Cognition and Behavior Reviews,* 4, 1-16. Retrieved from http://psyc.queensu.ca/ccbr/index.html

Magazine article

Nordhaus, T., & Shellenberger, M. (2009, May 20). The green bubble: Why environmentalism keeps imploding. *The New Republic*, 240(8), 16-18.

Magazine article, no author

Genocide step. (2009, June 3). *The New Republic 240(9)*, 1.

© 2009. Teacher's Discovery®

Online Magazine article

Xie, T. (2008, November 7). Physiology: Burn fat, live longer. *Science, 322,* 865-866. Retrieved from http://www.sciencemag.org /

Newsletter article, no author

Managing historic bridges in Arkansas. (2003, Spring). *Society for Industrial Archeology Newsletter, 32,* 14-15.

Daily newspaper article

Carson, S. (2009, May 23). How Boeing fights climate change. *Wall Street Journal,* p. A10.

Daily newspaper article, no author

Malaria, politics and DDT. (2009, May 23). *Wall Street Journal,* p. A10.

Daily newspaper, discontinuous pages

Weiss, J. (2004, March 27). Ads indicative of emotions in marriage debate. *Boston Globe,* pp. B1, B7.

Online newspaper article

Johnson, S. (2009, May 23). Stealth Starbucks: Seattle-based coffee giant opening neighborhood shops in disguise. *The Chicago Tribune.* Retrieved from http://www.chicagotribune.com

Weekly or bi-weekly newspaper article, letter to the editor

Schlesinger, Arthur, Jr. (2004, April 8). Disgrace at Guantanamo [Letter to the editor]. *New York Review of Books,* p. 85.

Review of a book

Finan, W.W. (2009). Hearts of darkness. [Review of the book *Africa's world war: Congo, the Rwandan genocide, and the making of a continental catastrophe,* by G. Prunier]. Current History 108(718), 235-237.

Review of a motion picture

Olszewski, T. (2009, May 22-28). All things sequel [Review of the motion picture *Night at the museum: Battle of the Smithsonian,* produced by Fox Films, 2009]. *Washington City Paper,* p. 38.

Monograph

Brainerd, C. J., Reyna, V. F., Howe, M. L., & Kingman, J. (1990). The development of forgetting and reminiscence. *Monograph of the Society for Child Research, 55* (3-4, Serial No. 222).

© 2009. Teacher's Discovery®

Abstract

Lahey, B. (2009). Public health significance of neuroticism. *American Psychologist, 64,* 241-256. Abstract retrieved from http://www.sciencedirect.com

Non-English journal article, title translated into English

Hong-Quan, L., & Lohoue, N. (2003) Estimations LP des solutions de l'equation des ondes sur certains variétés conique. [LP Estimates for solutions of the wave equation on certain conical varieties]. *Transactions of the American Mathematical Society,* 355, 689-711.

Books, Brochures, and Book Chapters

An entire book

Prochnik, G. (2006). *Putnam camp: Sigmund Freud, James Jackson Putnam, and the purpose of American psychology.* New York, NY: Other Press.

Book with multiple authors

Hauser, S., Allen, J. P., & Golden, E. (2006). *Out of the woods: Tales of resilient teens.* Cambridge, MA: Harvard University Press.

Electronic version of a print book

Fejes, A., & Nicoll, K. (Eds.) (2008). *Foucault and lifelong learning: Governing the subject.* [DX Reader version]. Retrieved from http://www.ebookstore.tandf.co.uk/html

Electronic-only book

Shrout, R. (n.d.). *True Hypnotism.* Retrieved from http://www.onlineoriginals.com

Book or brochure with a group author (government agency) as publisher

United States Fire Administration, Federal Emergency Management Agency. (2009). Get out and stay alive: A program for college campus and student fire safety. Retrieved from http://www.fema.gov/help/publications.shtm

Article or chapter in an edited book

Lindsay, R. A. (2008). Embryonic stem cell research is ethical. In V. Wagener (Ed.), *Biomedical ethics: Opposing viewpoints series.* (pp. 32-42). Detroit, MI: Greenhaven Press.

Grisso, T., and Appelbaum, P. S. (2003). Is it unethical to offer predictions of future violence? In D. N. Bersoff (Ed.), *Ethical conflicts in psychology* (3rd ed., pp. 499- 505). Washington, DC: American Psychological Association.

© 2009. Teacher's Discovery®

Entry in an encyclopedia or dictionary

Workman, J. R. (2006). Aristotle. In *Encyclopedia Americana international edition* (Vol. 2, pp. 73-76). New York, NY: Scholastic.

Shun, K. L. (2003). Moral psychology. In A. S. Cua (Ed.), *The encyclopedia of Chinese philosophy.* (475-479). New York, NY: Routledge.

Entry in an online encyclopedia or dictionary

Determinism. (n.d). *In Merriam-Webster's online dictionary* (11th Ed.). Retrieved from http://www.merriam-webster.com/dictionary/determinism

English translation of a book

Shantideva. (2006). *The way of the Bodhisattva.* (Padmarkara Translation Group, Trans.). Boston, MA: Shambhala Library.

Technical and Research Reports

American Physical Society. (2004). *Report of the American Physical Society study group on boost-phase intercept systems for national missile defense. Suppl. to Reviews of Modern Physics.*

National Institute of Justice. (2003, September). *Eyewitness evidence: A trainer's manual for law enforcement.* Special report by Technical Working Group for Eyewitness Evidence (NCJ Publication 188678). Washington, DC: Author.

U.S. Department of Health and Human Services, National Institutes of Health, National Heart, Lung, and Blood Institute. (2008). *How asthma-friendly is your school?* (NIH Publication No. 55-803). Retrieved from http://www.nhlbi.nih.gov/health/public/lung/asthma/friendhi.htm

Regularly published proceedings of meetings

Manson, N. C. (2003). Freud's own blend: Functional analysis, ideographic explanation, and the extension of ordinary psychology. *Proceedings of the Aristotelian Society, NS, 103,* 179-195.

Unpublished paper presented at a meeting

Baker, C. H. (2004, February 21). An existentialist take on American foreign policy. Paper presented at a meeting of the Washington Philosophy Club, Washington, DC.

Mahadevan, J. (2004, April 2). Conceptions of power influencing intercultural communication: The Southeast Asian perspective. Paper presented to the 2004 Congress of the Society for Intercultural Education, Training and Research, Berlin, Germany.

© 2009. Teacher's Discovery®

Audiovisual Media

Film

American Psychological Association (Producer). (2002). *Reclaiming hope in a changing world* [videocassette]. (Available from http://www.apa.org.videos/)

Skoll, J. & Guggenheim, D. (Producers), & Guggenheim, D. (Director). (2006). *An inconvenient truth* [Motion picture]. United States: Paramount Classics.

Television broadcast

Dugan, D. (Writer, Director). (2009, June 9). Lord of the ants [Television broadcast]. In P. Apsell, *Nova*. Boston, MA: Public Broadcasting Service.

Music recording

Helps, R. (2009). Symphony no. 1: Adagio. [Recorded by University of South Florida Symphony Orchestra]. On *Orchestral Works*. [CD]. Albany, NY: Albany Records.

Audio recording

Markos, L. (Speaker). (2000). Structuralism—Saussure and Levi-Strauss. Part 6, lecture 72 of *Great minds of the Western tradition* [Cassette recording]. Chantilly, VA: The Teaching Company.

Step 10 Summary

To prepare either MLA formatted Works Cited page or the APA References page:

- Arrange source cards in alphabetical order and list the entries in that order.

- Observe MLA or APA rules for formatting, capitalization, punctuation, abbreviations, and order for each entry.

- Follow the rules for each type of entry—e.g., book, article, database, etc.

- Make sure that the works cited entries correspond to the parenthetical citations.

- Double-space throughout.

- Check all entries for accuracy and completeness of information and for correctness of form.

© 2009. Teacher's Discovery®

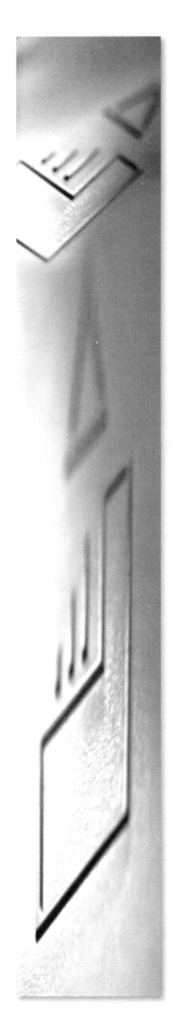

Appendix A

Reproducible Materials*

Contents

*Limited License Agreement: For each purchased copy of this work, a limited license is granted to allow reproduction of worksheets, forms, reference sheets, and checklists to one user. All reproducible pages are found within Appendix A.

Name: _____ Date: _____

Making a Plan

Understanding each of the steps, and the tasks involved in completing each one, allows the researcher to set reasonable deadlines so that work moves forward in a steady, deliberate way. Naturally, the amount of time required for any one step will vary according to the specific demands of a particular assignment and an individual's skill set. In addition, the steps are not actually discrete, but blend and overlap so that many tasks are actually on-going through continuous steps. For these reasons the researcher should always plan each project anew, instead of relying on a formula to guide deadline decisions.

Consider the final due date first, and use that to establish reasonable deadlines for each part of the process.

		Plan of Action	
Due Date		**Step**	**Decription**
	1	Understand the available resources.	Review types of resources, visit the school library, explore public and university library catalogues, and understand how to avoid plagiarism.
	2	Select a topic.	Find a topic, read reference materials to get a general overview of your topic, determine an angle, and narrow the topic to suit the assignment.
	3	Do preliminary research and begin writing source cards.	Locate valuable sources of information for your narrowed topic, read for ideas about thesis and topic headings, and record data about valuable resources on source cards.
	4	Formulate a thesis statement.	Propose a judgment, criticism, or evaluation about your topic, and identify the main topics which will support this tentative thesis.
	5	Make a tentative topic outline.	Continue researching and recording information on source cards, find specific supporting evidence for your main topics, and create a tentative outline to guide your note taking.
	6	Take notes.	Continue finding sources and recording information on source cards, but begin strategically selecting specific and relevant information to record on note cards.
	7	Extend topic outline.	Return to your tentative topic outline, revise thesis, write topic sentences for body sections, and fill in subtopics and supporting evidence with information from your note cards.
	8	Write rough draft.	Compose your paper, incorporating and citing your research, as well as your own insight and analysis.
	9	Edit and revise.	Re-read your paper and make corrections, ask others to read your paper and provide feedback, use the checklist to ensure that your writing is strong and your citations are correct.
	10	Prepare works cited page.	Consult the forms provided or use the MLA/APA handbooks for guidance, and prepare according to correct procedures a works cited or reference page listing the works actually used in your paper.
		Submit your paper on time and with pride, knowing that it is your best work.	

© 2009. Teacher's Discovery®

LLA: Reproducible for one user only.

Name: _____ Date: _____

Taking Notes: "Getting Stupid" Exercise Worksheets

Task 1. Help Mark find useful information. Begin by reading the article on the next four pages titled "Getting Stupid," by Bernice Wuethrich. The paragraphs have been numbered for easy reference. With a highlighter, pen, or pencil, specify the sections of the article that Mark might find useful for his paper. Look for both short-term and long-term effects, and for effects on both body and mind, as they pertain to teens. Identify these highlighted sections with brief headings and notes. Use these abbreviations:

ST for short-term effects
LT for long-term effects
Phys. for physical effects
Psych. for psychological effects

Ignore other information and details not immediately relevant to these topics.

Task 2. Now read the second version of the same article located on pages 58-61 to see how Mark's notes turned out. The paragraphs that Mark selected as relevant are highlighted, and his notes are located in the margins. Notice that, just as in the previous article, Mark has marked only those paragraphs that contain information about the effects of teenage drinking.

Task 3. Compare your "Getting Stupid" worksheet highlighting with Mark's, located on page 56, and see how it agrees. Bear in mind that annotating and highlighting are preliminary steps; what eventually ends up on the notes cards may change depending on what further reading uncovers.

Task 4. List under the topic headings below the information that belongs in each category.

Short-term Effects (both mind and body)	Long-term Effects (physical)	Long-term Effects (psychological)

LLA: Reproducible for one user only.

© 2009. Teacher's Discovery®

Getting Stupid

New research indicates that teenagers who drink too much may lose as much as 10 percent of their brainpower— the difference between passing and failing in school ... and in life

By Bernice Wuethrich

1   Sarah, a high school senior, drinks in moderation, but many of her friends do not. At one party, a classmate passed out after downing more than 20 shots of hard liquor and had to be rushed to a local emergency room. At another party a friend got sick, so Sarah made her drink water, dressed her in a sweatshirt to keep her warm, and lay her in bed, with a bucket on the floor. Then she brushed the girl's long hair away from her face so that it wouldn't get coated with vomit. "Every weekend, drinking is the only thing people do. Every single party has alcohol," says Sarah. (The names of the teenagers in these stories have been changed to protect their privacy.)

2   The most recent statistics from the U.S. Substance Abuse and Mental Health Services Administration's National Household Survey on Drug Abuse indicate that nearly 7 million youths between the ages of 12 and 20 binge-drink at least once a month. And despite the fact that many colleges have cracked down on drinking, Henry Wechsler of the Harvard School of Public Health says that two of every five college students still binge-drink regularly. For a male that means downing five or more drinks in a row; for a female it means consuming four drinks in one session at least once in a two-week period.

3   Few teens seem to worry much about what such drinking does to their bodies. Cirrhosis of the liver is unlikely to catch up with them for decades, and heart disease must seem as remote as retirement. But new research suggests that young drinkers are courting danger. Because their brains are still developing well into their twenties, teens who drink excessively may be destroying significant amounts of mental capacity in ways that are more dramatic than in older drinkers.

4   Scientists have long known that excessive alcohol consumption among adults over long periods of time can create brain damage, ranging from a mild loss of motor skills to psychosis and even the inability to form memories. But less has been known about the impact alcohol has on younger brains. Until recently, scientists assumed that a youthful brain is more resilient than an adult brain and could escape many of the worst ills of alcohol. But some researchers are now beginning to question this assumption. Preliminary results from several studies indicate that the younger the brain is, the more it may be at risk. "The adolescent brain is a developing nervous system, and the things you do to it can change it," says Scott Swartzwelder, a neuropsychologist at Duke University and the U.S. Department of Veterans Affairs.

5   Teen drinkers appear to be most susceptible to damage in the hippocampus, a structure buried deep in the brain that is responsible for many types of learning and memory, and the prefrontal cortex, located behind the forehead, which is the brain's chief decision maker and voice of reason. Both areas, especially the prefrontal cortex, undergo dramatic change in the second decade of life.

6   Swartzwelder and his team have been studying how alcohol affects the hippocampus, an evolutionarily old part of the brain that is similar in rats and humans. Six years ago, when Swartzwelder published his first paper suggesting that alcohol disrupts the hippocampus more severely in adolescent rats than in adult rats, "people didn't believe it," he says. Since then, his research has shown that the adolescent brain is more easily damaged in the structures that regulate the acquisition and storage of memories.

7   Learning depends on communication between nerve cells, or neurons, within the hippocampus. To communicate, a neuron fires an electrical signal down its axon, a single fiber extending away from the cell's center. In response, the axon releases chemical messengers, called neurotransmitters, which bind to receptors on the receiving branches of neighboring cells. Depending on the types of neurotransmitters released, the receiving cell may be jolted into action or settle more deeply into rest.

8   But the formation of memories requires more than the simple firing or inhibition of nerve cells. There must be some physical change in the hippocampal neurons that represents the encoding of new information. Scientists believe that this change occurs in the synapses, the tiny gaps between neurons that neurotransmitters traverse. Repeated use of synapses seems to increase their ability to fire up connecting cells. Laboratory experiments on brain tissue can induce this process, called long-term potentiation. Researchers assume that something similar takes place in the intact living brain, although it is impossible to observe directly. Essentially, if the repetitive neural reverberations

1

© 2009. Teacher's Discovery®
LLA: Reproducible for one user only.

are strong enough, they burn in new patterns of synaptic circuitry to encode memory, just as the more often a child recites his ABCs, the better he knows them.

9 Swartzwelder's first clue that alcohol powerfully disrupts memory in the adolescent brain came from studying rat hippocampi. He found that alcohol blocks long-term potentiation in adolescent brain tissue much more than in adult tissue. Next, Swartzwelder identified a likely explanation. Long-term potentiation— and thus memory formation— relies in large part on the action of a neurotransmitter known as glutamate, the brain's chemical king-pin of neural excitation. Glutamate strengthens a cell's electrical stimulation when it binds to a docking port called the NMDA receptor. If the receptor is blocked, so is long-term potentiation, and thus memory formation. Swartzwelder found that exposure to the equivalent of just two beers inhibits the NMDA receptors in the hippocampal cells of adolescent rats, while more than twice as much is required to produce the same effect in adult rats. These findings led him to suspect that alcohol consumption might have a dramatic impact on the ability of adolescents to learn. So he set up a series of behavioral tests.

10 First, Swartzwelder's team dosed adolescent and adult rats with alcohol and ran them through maze-learning tests. Compared with the adult rats, the adolescents failed miserably. To see whether similar results held true for humans, Swartzwelder recruited a group of volunteers aged 21 to 29 years old. He couldn't use younger subjects because of laws that forbid drinking before age 21. He chose to split the volunteers into two groups: 21 to 24 years old and 25 to 29 years old. "While I wouldn't argue that these younger folks are adolescents, even in their early twenties their brains are still developing," Swartzwelder says. After three drinks, with a blood-alcohol level slightly below the National Highway Traffic Safety Administration's recommended limit— .08 percent— the younger group's learning was impaired 25 percent more than the older group's.

11 Intrigued by these results, Swartzwelder's colleague Aaron White, a biological psychologist at Duke, set out to discover how vulnerable the adolescent brain is to long-term damage. He gave adolescent and adult rats large doses of alcohol every other day for 20 days— the equivalent of a 150-pound human chugging 24 drinks in a row. Twenty days after the last binge, when the adolescent rats had reached adulthood, White trained them in a maze-memory task roughly akin to that performed by a human when remembering the location of his car in a parking garage.

12 Both the younger and older rats performed equally well when sober. But when intoxicated, those who had binged as adolescents performed much worse. "Binge alcohol exposure in

adolescence appears to produce long-lasting changes in brain function," White says. He suspects that early damage caused by alcohol could surface whenever the brain is taxed. He also suspects that the NMDA receptor is involved, because just as alcohol in the system inhibits the receptor, the drug's withdrawal overstimulates it— which can kill the cell outright.

13 *During the fall semester last year, at least 11 college students died from alcohol-related causes— at California State University at Chico, Colgate University in New York, Old Dominion University in Virginia, the University of Michigan, Vincennes University in Kentucky, Washington and Lee University in Virginia, and Washington State University. No one knows how many other students were rushed to emergency rooms for alcohol poisoning, but at Duke, 11 students had visited local ERs in just the first three weeks of school, and in only one night of partying, three students from the University of Tennessee were hospitalized.*

14 Students who drink heavily sometimes joke that they are killing a few brain cells. New research suggests that this is not funny. Some of the evidence is anatomical: Michael De Bellis at the University of Pittsburgh Medical Center used magnetic resonance imaging to compare the hippocampi of subjects 14 to 21 years old who abused alcohol to the hippocampi of those who did not. He found that the longer and the more a young person had been drinking, the smaller his hippocampus. The average size difference between healthy teens and alcohol abusers was roughly 10 percent. That is a lot of brain cells.

15 De Bellis speculates that the shrinkage may be due to cell damage and death that occurs during withdrawal from alcohol. Withdrawal is the brain's way of trying to get back to normal after prolonged or heavy drinking. It can leave the hands jittery, set off the classic headache, generate intense anxiety, and even provoke seizures, as neurons that had adjusted to the presence of alcohol try to adjust to its absence. Because alcohol slows down the transmission of nerve signals— in part by stopping glutamate from activating its NMDA receptors— nerve cells under the influence react by increasing the number and sensitivity of these receptors. When drinking stops, the brain is suddenly stuck with too many hyperactive receptors.

16 Mark Prendergast, a neuroscientist at the University of Kentucky, recently revealed one way these hyperactive receptors kill brain cells. First, he exposed rat hippocampal slices to alcohol for 10 days, then removed the alcohol. Following withdrawal, he stained the tissue with a fluorescent dye that lit up dead and dying cells. When exposed to an alcohol concentration of about .08 percent, cell death increased some 25 percent above the

LLA: Reproducible for one user only.

© 2009. Teacher's Discovery®

baseline. When concentrations were two or three times higher, he wrote in a recent issue of Alcoholism: Clinical and Experimental Research, the number of dead cells shot up to 100 percent above the baseline.

17   Prendergast says that the younger brain tissue was far more sensitive. Preadolescent tissue suffered four to five times more cell death than did adult tissue. In all cases, most of the death occurred in hippocampal cells that were packed with NMDA receptors. To home in on the cause, he treated another batch of brain slices with the drug MK-801, which blocks NMDA receptors. He reasoned that if overexcitability during alcohol withdrawal was causing cell death, blocking the receptors should minimize the carnage. It did, by about 75 percent.

18   Now Prendergast is examining what makes the receptors so lethal. By tracking radioactive calcium, he found that the overexcited receptors open floodgates that allow calcium to swamp the cell. Too much calcium can turn on suicide genes that cause the neuron to break down its own membrane. Indeed, that is exactly what Prendergast observed during alcohol withdrawal: Overactive receptors opened wide, and the influx of calcium became a raging flood.

19   Prendergast says that four or five drinks may cause a mild withdrawal. And, according to Harvard's Wechsler, 44 percent of college students binge in this manner. More alarming, 23 percent of them consume 72 percent of all the alcohol that college students drink.

20   *Chuck was 15 the first time he binged— on warm beers chugged with friends late at night in a vacant house. Six years later, celebrating his 21st birthday, he rapidly downed four shots of vodka in his dorm room. Then he and his friends drove through the snowy night to a sorority party at a bar, where he consumed another 16 drinks. Chuck's friends later told him how the rest of the night unfolded. He danced in a cage. He spun on the floor. He careened around the parking lot with a friend on his back. Halfway home, he stumbled out of the car and threw up. A friend half carried him home down frozen roads at 2 a.m. "I don't remember any of this," Chuck says. But he does remember the hangover he lived with for two days, as his brain and body withdrew from the booze.*

21   Recent human studies support a conclusion Prendergast drew from his molecular experiments: The greatest brain damage from alcohol occurs during withdrawal. At the University of California at San Diego and the VA San Diego Health Care System, Sandra Brown, Susan Tapert, and Gregory Brown have been following alcohol-dependent adolescents for eight years. Repeated testing shows that problem drinkers perform more poorly on tests of cognition and learning than do nondrinkers. Furthermore, "the single best predictor of neuropsychological deficits for adolescents is withdrawal symptoms," says principal investigator Sandra Brown.

22   The psychologists recruited a group of 33 teenagers aged 15 and 16, all heavy drinkers. On average, each teen had used alcohol more than 750 times— the equivalent of drinking every day for two and a half years. Bingeing was common: The teens downed an average of eight drinks at each sitting. The researchers matched drinkers with nondrinkers of the same gender and similar age, IQ, socioeconomic background, and family history of alcohol use. Then, three weeks after the drinkers had their last drink, all the teens took a two-hour battery of tests.

23   The teens with alcohol problems had a harder time recalling information, both verbal and nonverbal, that they had learned 20 minutes earlier. Words such as apple and football escaped them. The performance difference was about 10 percent. "It's not serious brain damage, but it's the difference of a grade, a pass or a fail," Tapert says. Other tests evaluated skills needed for map learning, geometry, or science. Again, there was a 10 percent difference in performance.

24   "The study shows that just several years of heavy alcohol use by youth can adversely affect their brain functions in ways that are critical to learning," Sandra Brown says. She is following the group of teenagers until they reach age 30, and some have already passed 21. "Those who continue to use alcohol heavily are developing attentional deficits in addition to the memory and problem-solving deficits that showed up early on," Brown says. "In the past we thought of alcohol as a more benign drug. It's not included in the war on drugs. This study clearly demonstrates that the most popular drug is also an incredibly dangerous drug."

25   Brown's research team is also using functional magnetic resonance imaging to compare the brain function of alcohol abusers and nondrinkers. Initial results show that brains of young adults with a history of alcohol dependence are less active than the brains of nondrinkers during tasks that require spatial working memory (comparable to the maze task that White conducted on rats). In addition, the adolescent drinkers seem to exhibit greater levels of brain activity when they are exposed to alcohol-related stimuli. For instance, when the drinkers read words such as wasted or tequila on a screen, the nucleus accumbens— a small section of the brain associated with craving— lights up.

26   The nucleus accumbens is integral to the brain's socalled pleasure circuit, which scientists now believe undergoes major remodeling during adolescence. Underlying the pleasure circuit is the neurotransmitter dopamine. Sex, food, and

© 2009. Teacher's Discovery®   LLA: Reproducible for one user only.

many drugs, including alcohol, can all induce the release of dopamine, which creates feelings of pleasure and in turn encourages repetition of the original behavior. During adolescence, the balance of dopamine activity temporarily shifts away from the nucleus accumbens, the brain's key pleasure and reward center, to the prefrontal cortex. Linda Spear, a developmental psychobiologist at Binghamton University in New York, speculates that as a result of this shift in balance, teenagers may find drugs less rewarding than earlier or later in life. And if the drugs produce less of a kick, more will be needed for the same effect. "In the case of alcohol, this may lead to binge drinking," she says.

27   *When Lynn was a freshman in high school, she liked to hang out at her friend John's apartment. More often than not, his father would be drinking beer. "He was like, 'Help yourself,'" Lynn says. Friends would come over and play drinking games until four or five in the morning. The longer the games continued, the tougher the rules became, doubling and tripling the number of drinks consumed. One night, Lynn came home drunk. Her mother talked her through her options, sharing stories of relatives who had ruined their lives drinking. Lynn struggled with her choices. A year later she still drinks, but she's kept a pact with her girlfriends to stop bingeing.*

28   During adolescence, the prefrontal cortex changes more than any other part of the brain. At around age 11 or 12, its neurons branch out like crazy, only to be seriously pruned back in the years that follow. All this tumult is to good purpose. In the adult brain, the prefrontal cortex executes the thought processes adolescents struggle to master: the ability to plan ahead, think abstractly, and integrate information to make sound decisions.

29   Now there is evidence that the prefrontal cortex and associated areas are among those most damaged in the brains of bingeing adolescents. Fulton Crews, director of the Center for Alcohol Studies at the University of North Carolina at Chapel Hill, has studied the patterns of cell death in the brains of adolescent and adult rats after four-day drinking bouts. While both groups showed damage in the back areas of the brain and in the frontally located olfactory bulb, used for smell, only the adolescents suffered brain damage in other frontal areas.

30   That youthful damage was severe. It extended from the rat's olfactory bulb to the interconnected parts of the brain that process sensory information and memories to make associations, such as "This smell and the sight of that wall tell me I'm in a place where I previously faced down an enemy." The regions of cell death in the rat experiment corresponded to the human prefrontal cortex and to parts of the limbic system.

31   The limbic system, which includes the hippocampus, changes throughout adolescence, according to recent work by Jay Giedd at the National Institute of Mental Health in Bethesda, Maryland. The limbic system not only encodes memory but is also mobilized when a person is hungry or frightened or angry; it helps the brain process survival impulses. The limbic system and the prefrontal cortex must work in concert for a person to make sound decisions.

32   Damage to the prefrontal cortex and the limbic system is especially worrisome because they play an important role in the formation of an adult personality. "Binge drinking could be making permanent long-term changes in the final neural physiology, which is expressed as personality and behavior in the individual," Crews says. But he readily acknowledges that such conclusions are hypothetical. "It's very hard to prove this stuff. You can't do an experiment in which you change people's brains."

33   Nonetheless, evidence of the vulnerability of young people to alcohol is mounting. A study by Bridget Grant of the National Institute on Alcohol Abuse and Alcoholism shows that the younger someone is when he begins to regularly drink alcohol, the more likely that individual will eventually become an alcoholic. Grant found that 40 percent of the drinkers who got started before age 15 were classified later in life as alcohol dependent, compared with only 10 percent of those who began drinking at age 21 or 22. Overall, beginning at age 15, the risk of future alcohol dependence decreased by 14 percent with each passing year of abstention.

34   The study leaves unanswered whether early regular drinking is merely a marker of later abuse or whether it results in long-term changes in the brain that increase the later propensity for abuse. "It's got to be both," Crews says. For one thing, he points out that studies of rats and people have shown that repeated alcohol use makes it harder for a person— or a rat— to learn new ways of doing things, rather than repeating the same actions over and over again. In short, the way alcohol changes the brain makes it increasingly difficult over time to stop reaching for beer after beer after beer.

35   Ultimately, the collateral damage caused by having so many American adolescents reach for one drink after another may be incalculable. "People in their late teens have been drinking heavily for generations. We're not a society of idiots, but we're not a society of Einsteins either," says Swartzwelder. "What if you've compromised your function by 7 percent or 10 percent and never known the difference?"

Bernice Wuethrich/©2001.
Reprinted with permission of Discover Magazine.

LLA: Reproducible for one user only.   © 2009. Teacher's Discovery®

Name: _____ Date: _____

Website Evaluation Form

1. **What is the URL?** (Uniform Resource Locator or the address of the website)

    http:// _____

2. **What is the top-level domain?** This suffix tells you something about the producer of the site: a company (.com), university or museum (.edu), government (.gov), military (.mil), network (.net), non-profit organization (.org), or country, for example, Canada (.ca), or Latvia (.lv).

    .com _____ .edu _____ .gov _____ .mil _____ .net _____ .org _____ other _____ (.biz, .tv, .info)

3. **What is the complete title of the website?**

    Title of the website: _____

4. **Who is the authority for this site?** (author, editor, organization or institution name)

    Authority: _____

    On the appropriate line, write the name of the institution with which the author, editor, or institution is associated.

    k12 school _____ university _____

    govt. agency _____ organization _____

    company _____ other _____

    Can you contact this site? yes _____ no _____ How? _____

5. **What is the content of the site?**

    Does this site provide text only? yes _____ no _____

    Does it provide text with graphics? yes _____ no _____ Multimedia? yes _____ no _____

    Do the graphics and/or multimedia contribute to the topic? yes _____ no _____

    Does the site include advertising? yes _____ no _____

    Is the material at this site primary/secondary/? yes _____ no _____

6. **What is the primary purpose of the site?**

    Inform _____ Persuade _____ Provide facts _____ Offer opinions _____

    Does the site have a clear political or philosophical agenda? yes _____ no _____

    If yes, what is the site's ideological slant? _____

    Political agenda: _____

7. **How current is the site?**

    When was this page written or last updated? _____

    Are the links active? _____ Are they useful? _____

8. **How would you rate this Web page?** Add your own comments.

    Use with caution _____ Good basic information _____ Excellent for this assignment _____

   LLA: Reproducible for one user only.

Name: _____　Date: _____

Topic Outline for a Research Paper

Thesis Statement: _____
_____

Topic Sentence for First Major Topic: _____
_____

Specific Examples, Details

Support ⎧ a. _____
⎨ b. _____
⎩ c. _____

Topic Sentence for Second Major Topic: _____
_____

Specific Examples, Details

Support ⎧ a. _____
⎨ b. _____
⎩ c. _____

Topic Sentence for Third Major Topic: _____
_____

Specific Examples, Details

Support ⎧ a. _____
⎨ b. _____
⎩ c. _____

LLA: Reproducible for one user only.　　© 2009. Teacher's Discovery®

Name: _____ Date: _____

Position Paper Outline

A. Introduction

    1. Issue: _____

    2. Significance: _____

    3. Thesis statement: _____

B. Arguments against your position (Counterarguments)

    1. _____

    2. _____

    3. _____

    4. _____

C. Arguments in favor of your position

    1. _____

    2. _____

    3. _____

    4. _____

D. Conclusion

    1. Restatement of thesis statement: _____

        _____

    2. Ideas for going beyond it: _____

        _____

LLA: Reproducible for one user only.

MLA at a Glance Reference Sheets

MLA—Print Resources	
Books	**Example**
One Author Author's Last Name, First Name. *Title*. Place of publication: Publisher, date. Medium.	Pinker, Steven. *The Language Instinct: How the Mind Creates Language*. New York: Harper, 2007. Print.
Two Authors Author's Last Name, First Name, and 2nd Author's First Name and Last Name. *Title*. Place of publication: Publisher, date. Medium.	Frum, David and Richard Perle. *An End to Evil: How to Win the War on Terror*. New York: Random, 2004. Print.
More than three authors First author's Last Name, First Name, et al. *Title*. Place of publication: Publisher, date. Medium.	Jolly, Richard, et al. *UN Contributions to Development Thinking and Practice*. Bloomington: Indiana UP, 2004. Print.
Editor (ed.) Editor's Last Name, First Name, ed. *Title*. Place of publication: Publisher, date. Medium.	Wetmore, Kevin J., ed. *Revenge Drama in European Renaissance and Japanese Theater: From Hamlet to Madame Butterfly*. New York: Macmillan, 2008. Print.
Chapter, Article, Essay, Poem, Short Story in an Anthology or Compilation Author's Last Name, First Name. "Essay Title." Book Title. Ed. Editor's First and Last Name. Vol. number. ed. Place of publication: Publisher, date. Page numbers. Medium.	Truth, Sojourner. "Ar'n't I a Woman." *Norton Anthology of African American Literature*. Ed. Henry Louis Gates Jr. and Nellie Y. McKay. 2nd ed. New York: Norton, 2003. 196-198. Print.
Previously Published Article or Essay in a Book Author's Last Name, First Name. "Article Title." *Original Publication Title* volume.issue (date): pages. Rpt. in *Title of book*. Ed. First Name and Last Name. Vol. number. Place of publication: Publisher, date. Pages. Medium.	Williams, Carol T. "Nabokov's Dozen Short Stories: His World in Microcosm." *Studies in Short Fiction* 12 (1975): 213-22. Rpt. in *Twentieth Century American Literature*. Ed. Harold Bloom. Vol. 5. New York: Chelsea, 1987. 2807-11. Print.
Periodicals	**Example**
Magazine Article with an Author Author's Last Name, First Name. "Article Title." *Periodical Title* day Month year: page range. Medium. Note: magazines and newspapers do not require volume or issue number.	Hersh, Seymour M. "Torture at Abu Ghraib." *New Yorker* 10 May 2004: 42-47. Print.
Scholarly Journal Article with an Author Author's Last Name, First Name. "Article Title." *Periodical Title* volume.issue (day Month year): page range. Medium.	Matthews, Cameron. "A Higher Purpose: Profiles in Presidential Courage." *Presidential Studies Quarterly* 39.3 (Sept. 2009): 160-2. Print.
Print Encyclopedias, Reference Books	**Example**
Article in an Encyclopedia Author's Last Name, First Name. "Article Title." *Encyclopedia Title*. Edition. date. Medium.	Art, Robert J. "United Nations." *World Book*. 2001 ed. Print.
Article in a Specialized Reference Book (without an author) "Article Title." Reference Title. Ed. Editor's First and Last Name. Number of ed. Vol. number. Place of publication: Publisher, date. Medium.	"Archimedes." Encyclopedia of World Biography. Ed. Paula Byers. 2nd ed. Vol. 1. Detroit: Gale, 1998. Print.

© 2009. Teacher's Discovery®

MLA at a Glance Reference Sheets

MLA—Online Resources	
Works Cited Only on the Web	**Example**
A Web Page Author's Last Name, First Name. "Article Title." *Overall Website Title.* Publisher/sponsor of the site (if not available, use N.p.), Date (day month year; if not available use n.d.). Medium. Access date (day month year).	Ockerbloom, John Mark, ed. "Banned Books Online." *Online Books Page.* U of Penn., 22 May 2009. Web. 25 May 2009.
Article in Online Newspaper or Magazine Author's Last Name, First Name. "Article Title." *Overall Website title.* Version or edition. Publisher/sponsor of the site (if not available, use N.p.), Date (day month year; if not available use n.d.). Medium. Access date (day month year).	Sayle, Carol Ann."The Downside of Year-Round Farming." *The Atlantic.com.* Atlantic Monthly Group, 25 May 2009. Web. 1 June 2009.
Online Encyclopedia Author's Last Name, First Name. "Article Title." *Encyclopedia Title.* Sponsor/Publisher of the site (if not available use N.p.), Date (day month year; if not available use n.d.). Medium. Access date (day month year).	"Aphrodite." *Encyclopaedia Britannica Online.* Encyclopaedia Britannica, 2009. Web. 6 May 2009.
Works Cited on the Web with Print Publication Data	**Example**
Article republished on the Web Author's Last Name, First Name. "Article Title." *Original Publication Title* date: page(s). *Title of website,* Sponsor of website, Date. Medium. Date of Access (day Month, year).	Douglass, Frederick. "Reconstruction." *Atlantic Monthly* 1866: 71-75. *Electronic Text Center.* U. of Virginia Library, Feb. 1994. Web. 31 Jan. 2008.
Short story or poem republished on the Web Author's Last Name, First Name. "Poem/Story Title." *Original Book Title.* Ed. Editor First Name and Last Name. Publication Location: Company, Date. *Website Title.* Sponsor, date. Medium. Access date (day Month year).	Dickenson, Emily. "I like to see it lap the miles." *Complete Poems of Emily Dickinson.* Ed. Steven van Leeuwen. Boston: Little, 1924. *Great Books Online.* Bartleby.com, 2000. Web. 20 Mar. 2004.
Subscription Service Databases	**Example**
Periodical from an Online Database Author's Last Name, First Name. "Article Title." *Periodical Title* volume number.issue number (day month year): page range. *Title of Database.* Medium. Access date (day, Month, year).	Gornek, Vivian. "Trying to Get Their Own Back." *Women's Review of Books* 20.2 (Nov. 2007): 6. *Student Resource Center Gold.* Web. 26 May 2009.
CD-ROM or DVD-ROM	**Example**
CD-ROM or DVD-ROM Author's Last Name, First Name. "Article Title." *Publication Title.* Edition, release, or version. Place of publication: Name of publisher, Date of publication. Medium.	"Pandora." *Oxford English Dictionary.* 2nd ed. Vers. 4.0. Oxford: Oxford UP, 2007. CD-ROM.

 LLA: Reproducible for one user only.

APA at a Glance Reference Sheets

APA—Print Resources	
Books	**Example**
One Author Author's Last Name, First & Second Initial. (Date). *Title.* City of publication, State abbreviation: Publisher.	Prochnik, G. (2006). *Putnam camp: Sigmund Freud, James Jackson Putnam, and the purpose of American psychology.* New York, NY: Other Press.
Two Authors Author's Last Name, First & Second Initial, & 2nd Author's Last Name, First & Second Initial. (Date). *Title.* City of publication, State abbreviation: Publisher. [Give names, initials of up to seven authors].	Spangenburg, R., & Moser, D. K. (1993). *The history of science from the ancient Greeks to the scientific revolution.* New York, NY: Facts on File.
Editor (ed.) Editor's Last Name, First & Second Initial. (Ed.). (Date). *Title.* City of publication, State abbreviation: Publisher.	Lim, S. (Ed.). (2000). *Asian-American literature: An anthology.* New York, NY: McGraw-Hill.
Periodicals	**Example**
With an Author Author's Last Name, First & Second Initial. (year, Month day). Article title. *Periodical Title, volume*(issue), page range.	Kruesi, L. (2009). Astronomers capture meager spiral. *Astronomy, 37*(6), 42-47.
With Multiple Authors [For listing the authors' names, follow the instructions above for 2-6 authors]. (year, Month day). Article title. Periodical Title, volume(issue), page range.	Nelson, D. R., Hammen, C., Brennan, P. A., & Ullman, J. B. (2003, October). The impact of maternal depression on adolescent adjustment: The role of expressed emotion. Journal of Counseling and Clinical Psychology, 71, 935-944.
Without an Author Article title. (year, Month day). *Periodical Title, volume*(issue), page range.	Vietnamese Americans: Lessons in American history. (2004, Spring). *Teaching Tolerance, 25,* 31-35.
Print Encyclopedias, Reference Books	**Example**
With an Author Author's Last Name, First & Second Initial. (Date). Article title. In *Encyclopedia title* (Vol., page range). City of publication, State abbreviation: Publisher.	Rook, K. S. (2000). Loneliness. In A. E. Kazden (Ed.), *Encyclopedia of psychology* (Vol. 5, pp. 73-76). New York, NY: Oxford University Press.
Without an Author Article Title. (Date). In *Encyclopedia title* (Vol., page range). City of Publication, State abbreviation: Publisher.	United Nations. (2000). In *Columbia encyclopedia* (6th ed., pp. 2826-2828). New York, NY: Columbia University Press.

© 2009. Teacher's Discovery®

APA at a Glance Reference Sheets

APA—Online Resources	
Online Periodicals (including articles from databases)	**Example**
Article in Online Newspaper Author's Last Name, First & Second Initial. (year, Month day). Article title. *Periodical title*. Retrieved from URL	Klein, A. (2009, July 20). Drop in crime rate unexpected. *Washington Post*. Retrieved from http://www.washingtonpost.com
Article in Online Magazine Author's Last Name, First & Second Initial. (year, Month day). Article title. *Periodical title*. Retrieved from URL	Boutin, P. (2004, March). The case for staying off Mars. *Wired magazine*. Retrieved from http://www.wired.com/wired/archive/12.03/start.html?pg=14
Online Journal Article with DOI Author's Last Name, First & Second Initial. (year, Month day). Article title. *Periodical title, volume*(issue), pages. doi: number	Ward, T., & Salmon, K. (2009). The ethics of punishment: Correctional practice implications. *Aggression and Violent Behavior*, 14(4): 239-247. doi: 10.1016/j.avb.2009.03.009
Online Journal Article without DOI Author's Last Name, First & Second Initial. (year, Month day). Article title. *Periodical title, volume*(issue), pages. Retrieved from URL	Crystal, J. D., & Foote, A. L. (2009). Metacognition in Animals. *Comparative Cognition & Behavior Reviews, 4*, 1-16. Retrieved from http://psyc.queensu.ca/ ccbr/index.html
Internet Sites	**Example**
With an Author Author's Last Name, First & Second Initials. (year, Month day). Article or section title. In *Title of Internet site or Web page*. Retrieved from URL	Gray, T. A. (2009, May 26). A Shakespeare timeline. In *Mr. William Shakespeare and the Internet*. Retrieved from http://shakespeare.palomar.edu/timeline/timeline.htm
Without an Author Article title. (Date). In *Title of Internet site or Web page*. Retrieved from URL	Black death, 1348. (2004) In *Eyewitness to history*. Retrieved from http://www.eyewitnesstohistory.com/plague.htm
Online Encyclopedias, Reference Works	**Example**
With an Author Author's Last Name, First & Second Initial. (Date). Article title. In *Encyclopedia Title* (version or edition). Retrieved from URL	Alexander, J. M. (2009). Evolutionary game theory. In E. N. Zalta (Ed.) *The Stanford encyclopedia of philosophy* (Fall 2009 ed.) Retrieved from http://plato.stanford.edu/ archives/fall2009/entries/game-evolutionary/
Without an Author Article title. (Date). In *Encyclopedia Title* (version or edition). Retrieved from URL	Landscape architecture. (2004). In *Encyclopedia Britannica*. Retrieved from http://www.Britannica.com/eb/article?eu=48157

 LLA: Reproducible for one user only.

Proofreading at a Glance

Individual teachers, schools, style manuals, and dictionaries all suggest different ways to indicate errors in written work. The notation given here includes symbols that many teachers and students find useful as shorthand to mark errors and suggest improvements. Examples follow the error or writing weakness when appropriate.

Usages	Symbol	Example
Spelling error	sp	We woud like more broccoli. [would]
Close up space; print as one word	⌒	Every body; basket ball.
Delete, or word crossed out; take it out	ℓ	The squirrels up in our attic are an annoying nuisance.
Insert missing word or needed punctuation	∧	The troll at the bridge would not let pass. the goats
Insert space	#	Afterschool, we headed for GreatFalls.
Transpose elements; change the order	∽	recieve; After a many sleepless night
Punctuation error(s)	ρ and ∧	Men women and children ran in all directions. The twins were chanting Ants! Ants! Ants wear underpants.
Use a lowercase letter	⌐C and /	I plan to study Sociology and Basket Weaving in College.
Capitalization error(s); use a capital letter	c, cap, and ≡	In english I'm reading a novel about indians.
Begin a new paragraph; indent	¶	… Vonnegut's novel *Slaughterhouse-Five* has been banned time after time. ¶Bruce Severy, a teacher at Drake High School in North Dakota who taught *Slaughterhouse-Five*, defended it …
Do not begin a new paragraph	no ¶	… Vonnegut's novel *Slaughterhouse-Five* has been banned time after time. no ¶ Bruce Severy, a teacher at Drake High School in North Dakota who taught *Slaughterhouse-Five*, defended it …

Symbol	Usages
shift/t	Shift from one tense to another—e.g., past to present.
shift/pov	Shift from one point of view to another—e.g., first person to third. Be consistent in the use of verb tenses and point of view.
?	Vague or ambiguous; make the meaning clear.
awk	Awkward; clumsy phrasing or sentence structure; rewrite sentence, striving for grace, balance, and clarity.
trans	Transition needed; provide transitional words or phrases to link ideas, sentences, and paragraphs.
coh	Problems with coherence; paragraph lacks unity and organization; does not hang together. Rethink the focus; re-examine the thesis statement (Th S), topic sentence (TS), and supporting ideas.

LLA: Reproducible for one user only.   © 2009. Teacher's Discovery®

Proofreading at a Glance

Usages	Symbol	Example
Sentence fragment or incomplete sentence; add the missing parts, often the main verb	frag	Because our teamwork was superior. Under the stairway, where no one had looked.
Run-on sentence, also called comma splice; two sentences run together with no punctuation or joined only by a comma; provide the correct punctuation	r-o	We're planning a party, we've invited everyone. Jane wrote the lyrics, Carlos composed the music.
Dangling or misplaced modifier; rearrange the sentence	dm mm	Racing toward the finish, a pothole made him stumble. Samantha saw a dog gnawing a bone on her way to school.

Usages	Symbol	Example
Faulty parallel structure; when presenting a series be consistent in the use of specific parts of speech, infinitives, and verbs	//	We held a bake sale, a car wash, and we sold raffle tickets. The club president's duties include planning the program, running the meetings, and to make sure that new members feel welcome.
Passive voice; make the verbs active; give the grammatical subject of the sentence the action	pv	Active: The aardvark ate my birthday cake. Passive: My birthday cake was eaten by the aardvark.
Lack of agreement between subject and verb (s-v) or between pronoun and antecedent (p-a); make both singular or both plural	agr	Neither Matthew nor Hannah know the answer. Everyone should open their books to page 17.
Wrong word; word does not have the meaning suggested	ww	He flaunted the rules until the principal expelled him. [The writer means *flout*, not *flaunt*].
Weak word choice; tone or level of language inappropriate	wc	A bunch of guys started harassing us kids; the thing about it was, the fight became pretty interesting.
Grammatical error	gr	Between you and I, she is a liar and a thief. When I saw him laying on the floor, I almost died.
Faulty logic	log	It's not true that smoking causes cancer; my grandfather smokes a pack a day and he's 85. The astronauts saw no angels in outer space, so obviously angels don't exist.
Wordiness	w	The alarm, which I set the night before, went off extremely early at 6 a.m. before the sun came up at dawn.
Needless repetition	rep	In Salinger's novel, Salinger shows many of the problems of adolescents and young people.
Redundancy	red	salty brine; hot water heater; pizza pie
Indefinite reference	ir or ref	As the creature emerged from the black lagoon, it was silent. [The reference of it is unclear].

 LLA: Reproducible for one user only.

Peer Feedback and Review Checklist

Name of Reviewer: _____   Name of Author: _____

Paper Title: _____   Date: _____

Record additional comments and/or notes on a separate piece of paper. Please use red, green, or blue ink for notations within the paper. Check off each step as it is completed.

Overview: Circle all instances where changes are required and make suggestions for corrections whenever possible.

_____ **Person**—Have first- or second- person pronouns (I, me, you, we, etc.) been omitted? Exception: when in direct quotes.

_____ **Tense**—Is literature always referred to in the present tense? Are historical events and scientific research experiments referred to in the past tense?

_____ **Quotations**—Has the author avoided the use of phrases like: *this quote means/indicates ...*?

_____ **Citations**—Are all citations completed correctly according to the required style guidelines?

_____ **Grammar**—Has the author used correct grammar throughout?

_____ **Weakness**—Are there any places where the writing shows weaknesses such as passive voice, vagueness, verbosity, redundancy, etc.?

Introductory Paragraph(s): Underline and label the sentence(s) with a colored pen.

_____ **Opening Statement**—Is there an opening statement that focuses the reader's attention and introduces the general subject?

_____ **Thesis Statement**—Does the thesis announce the main purpose of the essay and does the thesis propose an interesting topic worthy of discussion?

_____ **Method of Development**—Does the MOD clearly address at least two distinct topics that can be used to prove or further explain the thesis? Number these topics. Are these areas stated clearly? Do they blend well with the rest of the introductory paragraph?

Body Paragraphs: Follow instructions in each question.

_____ **Clear MOD**—Are there clear body sections covering the topics addressed in the MOD? Number these sections as they correspond to the MOD.

_____ **Topic Sentences**—Does each body paragraph contain a topic sentence that details the general idea of the paragraph and makes a clear connection to the thesis statement? Underline these sentences.

_____ **Support From Sources**—Does each body section contain paraphrases and direct quotes that are correctly cited and integrated into the paper's flow, with lead-ins and follow-ups?

_____ **Analysis**—Does the author fully, comprehensively, and clearly explain the connection between the borrowed material and the thesis statement?

Conclusion Paragraph(s): Follow instructions in each question.

_____ **New Ideas**—Does the conclusion paragraph present any new ideas not discussed previously? If so, cross them out or reassign them to appropriate body paragraphs.

_____ **MOD Restatement**—Does the conclusion include a restatement of the MOD? Underline this sentence.

_____ **Thesis Restatement**—Does the conclusion restate the thesis using different words? Underline this sentence.

_____ **Closure**—Does the conclusion bring closure to the paper and satisfaction to the reader?

    © 2009. Teacher's Discovery®

Name: _____ Date: _____

Peer Feedback and Review Checklist continued

Holistic Feedback: Be detailed in your responses.

Rate the strength of the paper's argument, and then provide comments that explain the ranking.

weak　　1　　2　　3　　4　　5　　strong

Comments:

Rate and explain how well the paper connects ideas and guides the reader through the analysis.

poorly　　1　　2　　3　　4　　5　　well

Comments:

Rate the organization of the paper, and then explain your ranking.

disorganized　　1　　2　　3　　4　　5　　organized

Comments:

Provide no fewer than three suggestions about how the author can improve the paper.

1.

2.

3.

© 2009. Teacher's Discovery®

LLA: Reproducible for one user only.

Research Paper Final Checklist

Formatting

_____ Readable 12-point typeface.
_____ 1-inch margins.
_____ Tab indent on paragraphs.
_____ Title is centered.
_____ Title uses upper & lower case letters.
_____ Proper title capitalization is used.
_____ No quotations or underlines used on title, unless naming a book or other title.

_____ One line is skipped after the title.
_____ No extra spaces after paragraphs.
_____ Text has been double-spaced throughout.
_____ Teacher instructions have been observed.
_____ Pagination is done correctly.
_____ Headings are done correctly.
_____ Running headers are done correctly.
_____ Cover page, if required, is correctly formatted.

Proofreading

_____ With each revision/change, spelling and grammar checks have been run and corrections made.
_____ The author has proofread the paper with every revision/change.
_____ The author has read the paper aloud.
_____ An additional person has proofread the paper.
_____ Strict attention has been paid to addressing all corrections, comments, and questions raised by teachers and/or peers.
_____ Grammar and usage are correct throughout.

_____ Consistency/continuity in verb usage.
_____ Consistency/continuity in point of view.
_____ Present tense for literature and literary criticism.
_____ Past tense for historical and scientific research experiment information.
_____ Third person is used in literary analysis and expository writing, except where appropriate.
_____ Correct punctuation is used.
_____ All titles are underlined, italicized, or have quotation marks as needed.

Works cited page/references

_____ Includes ALL works mentioned in the paper.
_____ Includes ONLY works mentioned in the paper.
_____ Entries are in alphabetical order.
_____ Capitalization is according to MLA/APA rules.

_____ Punctuation is according to MLA/APA rules.
_____ Entries correspond to the sources cited in-text.
_____ Entries correspond to sources on source cards.

Documentation & Use of Borrowed Material

_____ A variety of sources have been used.
_____ No one source has been relied on too heavily.
_____ Internet sources have been evaluated.

_____ All borrowed material is on the note cards.
_____ All sources can be produced on request.
_____ All sources are recorded on source cards.

Plagiarism has been avoided by

_____ paraphrasing in-text.
_____ placing direct quotes in quotation marks.
_____ accurately citing in-text documentation.
_____ showing omissions in quotes with ellipses.

_____ summarizing in-text.
_____ citing in the correct subject area format.
_____ checking all borrowed materials for proper use and accuracy.

Structure and Content

The thesis paragraph contains
_____ focusing sentences.
_____ thesis statement.
_____ method of development.

The body paragraphs have
_____ strong topic sentences.
_____ presented material supporting the thesis.
_____ transitions for smooth shifts.

Upon Final Review ...

_____ By completing this checklist, the author asserts that this research paper reflects his/her superior personal efforts.

Paper Title:_____ Signature: _____ Date: _____

LLA: Reproducible for one user only.   © 2009. Teacher's Discovery®

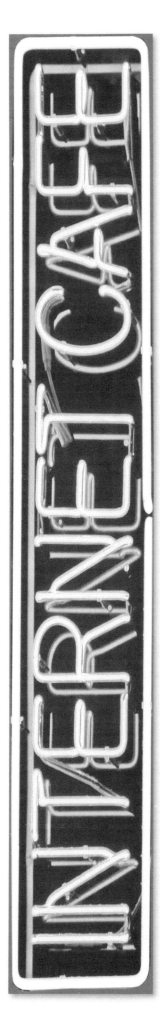

Appendix B

Using the Internet

Searching the Internet has become an increasingly important part of students' research projects. It contains valuable information, but it can also gobble up huge amounts of time. Although the scope of this book does not allow for a full exploration of how to effectively navigate the myriad tools and techniques that can make Internet searching profitable, this appendix does attempt to provide basic information that will facilitate a search. It deals briefly with the following topics: search engines, meta-search tools, subject directories, useful sites, and evaluation of Internet sources. When using this appendix, be aware that engines and sites are subject to rapid change that may affect the quality of the information that is retrieved. Make notations to this section by replacing defunct URLs with current ones, eliminating search engines that no longer fire up, and crossing out sites that no longer exist. Researchers require comprehensive information about current Internet searching techniques, tools, and sites.

Since different search engines have different capabilities, it's probably a mistake to lock onto just one search engine and to ignore all the rest. The same is true of meta-search tools, where, on a specific query, one engine may find 30 hits while another registers zero.

Subject directories are often the best place to start a search because in many cases human beings, rather than robots, spiders, and crawlers, have evaluated and categorized the sources. This can save time and can increase the likelihood that the material is reliable and authoritative. As noted below, a number of search engines are now combined with subject directories. This means researchers can search both the directory and the Web from a single site.

© 2009. Teacher's Discovery®

Search Engines

Search engines are software designed to look through an indexed database of Internet documents. They are the key to finding precisely the information that you want from the millions and millions of documents out there in cyberspace. All search engines offer help on their main page; most provide both basic and advanced searches, and many offer features such as spelling correction, searches by specific media, and subject directories. Because search engines operate using different formulas, don't rely on just one.

Note:

Search engines often provide many results that are paid placement or paid inclusion, and these results are not always clearly identified as such.

AllTheWeb   http://www.alltheweb.com

AltaVista   http://www.altavista.com

AltaVista is especially strong in finding foreign sites and information in foreign languages. By adding domain and the country abbreviation, you can search websites registered by country—e.g., add *domain:de* to your search term to find only German sites.

Ask.com   http://www.ask.com

Google   http://www.google.com

Gigablast.com   http://www.gigablast.com

Lycos   http://www.lycos.com

MSN Search   http://www.msn.com

Live Search   http://www.live.com

Scirus   http://scirus.com

Scirus searches only science content on the Web and includes links to scholarly journals and peer-reviewed articles.

Yahoo!   http://www.yahoo.com

Yahoo also has a search engine specifically designed for k-12 research: *http://education.yahoo.com/*. Resources include a Spanish/English dictionary, Bartlett's Familiar Quotations, WorldFactbook, The Oxford Shakespeare, and Gray's Anatomy.

© 2009. Teacher's Discovery®

Meta-Search Tools

A meta-search tool allows you to submit your query to several search engines at the same time and then combines the results onto one page. Meta-search engines often turn up obscure sources that other engines miss. They allow you to preview what a broad search will involve. Although there are a number of meta-search engines, we will list only a few of the most popular ones.

Clusty http://clusty.com

Clusty groups responses into topics, which you can then search from general to more specific. It also includes a blog search function.

Dogpile http://www.dogpile.com

Ixquick http://ixquick.com

Kartoo http://kartoo.com

This meta-searcher returns results with a visual snapshot of the page. While the screen can be difficult to read, this makes eliminating irrelevant pages somewhat easier.

Mamma http://www.mamma.com

Surfwax http://www.surfwax.com

Subject Directories

Subject directories are a good place to start your search because they organize websites into categories and subcategories that include information that librarians and other experts consider important and useful. While they include fewer websites than a search engine, the featured websites tend to be more useful.

About.com http://www.about.com

Infomine http://infomine.ucr.edu

Infomine provides a scholarly collection of directories on the Web, with search by keyword or academic discipline.

Librarians Index to the Internet http://lii.org

The directory is constantly updated and provides only material that has been reviewed and evaluated for substance and reliability, making it one of the top choices among academically oriented directories.

Academic Info http://www.academicinfo.net/subject-guides

Open Directory Project http://www.dmoz.org

Open Directory is the largest human-edited directory on the Web. It models itself on the Oxford English Dictionary, depending on some 35,000 volunteer editors with expertise in specific areas.

© 2009. Teacher's Discovery®

Starting Points: Some Useful Sites

There are now thousands of useful sites on the Internet, depending on the research topic. Here we will list only a handful of sites that have proved especially useful to student researchers. Many of these sites will lead to other, equally useful sites.

News and Current Events

The three newspapers below all have a fee-based archive for older articles and a free retrieval service for recent ones. All provide reliable, carefully researched material as well as some special features for online users. Many other newspapers are available online, but most experts consider these to be the best.

Los Angeles Times	**http://www.latimes.com**
New York Times	**http://www.nytimes.com**
Washington Post	**http://www.washingtonpost.com**
NewsLink	**http://newslink.org**

This site allows searches by region and newspaper.

Another excellent source of news is radio and television. All the major networks have websites, and they are especially good for late-breaking news. Two noteworthy sites are described below.

CNN Interactive	**http://www.cnn.com**
National Public Radio	**http://www.npr.org**

Good for in-depth coverage of important issues and events.

Libraries

The Internet Public Library **http://www.ipl.org**

Users can search for information under subject categories or in the Reference Center, which includes many full-text books, including almanacs, dictionaries, encyclopedias, atlases, and other reference works. The Reading Room is a gateway to hundreds of online books, magazines, and newspapers.

Library of Congress **http://www.loc.gov**

It is the national collection of books, country studies, historical documents and photographs, databases, catalogs, and Internet links. Under Collections & Services users can search the online catalogue for over 12 million items: books, serials, files, manuscripts, maps, and audio and visual materials.

National Library of Medicine **http://www.nlm.nih.gov**

The National Library of Medicine is the world's largest medical library. It provides information and links about medical topics in the news, diseases, drugs, journals, and exhibitions.

WWW Virtual Library **http://www.vlib.org**

Look for information organized by disciplines and categories, where there are links to many full-text books and articles from a variety of sources

© 2009. Teacher's Discovery®

Information Sources for Specific Disciplines

Literature, Arts, and Humanities

Bartleby: Great Books Online   http://www.bartleby.com

Bartleby's list of online publications includes literature, both fiction and nonfiction, reference, and poetry, all available without charge. Reference books include The Columbia Encyclopedia, American Heritage Dictionary, Bartlett's Familiar Quotations, Roget's II: The New Thesaurus, Cambridge History of English and American Literature (18 vols), and Gray's Anatomy.

Cleveland Press
Shakespeare Photographs 1870–1982   http://www.ulib.csuohio.edu/shakespeare

This site has remarkable production photography of Shakespeare's plays, including stage, film, TV, opera, and ballet versions.

Literary Resources on the Net   http://andromeda.rutgers.edu/~jlynch/Lit/

Provides links to academic web pages, scholarly projects, and articles on the Web covering a variety of genres, authors, themes, and time periods in British and American literature.

Mr. William Shakespeare and the Internet   http://shakespeare.palomar.edu

An annotated guide to scholarly Shakespeare resources on the Internet, this site also lists many links to texts, criticism, study guides, and the like.

Web Gallery of Art   http://www.wga.hu/index1.html

This site, specializing in European art of the Gothic, Baroque, and Renaissance periods, contains over 10,000 images. It is searchable by artist, time period, or medium.

World Wide Arts Resource   http://www.wwar.com

This site includes art news, links to images, and information about art movements in history and artist biographies. Also includes many contemporary artists.

Here are two additional sites that provide links and access to thousands of full-text books, poems, plays, essays, and a variety of other publications.

Electronic Text Center at the University of Virginia   http://etext.lib.virginia.edu

Project Gutenberg   http://www.gutenberg.net

© 2009. Teacher's Discovery®

Science

NASA   http://www.nasa.gov

This site is a source of the latest news and information about NASA science, technology, and strategic enterprises, covering life on earth, humans in space, and exploring the universe. There are special resources for students and educators.

National Institutes of Health   http://health.nih.gov

Provides information about clinical trials, drugs, special programs, and a vast array of specific illnesses and health problems. Connects to Medline, Healthfinder, and many other resources.

Nature   http://www.nature.com/nature

Offers free online articles on a range of scientific topics in publications from the Nature Publishing Group.

Scholarpedia   http://www.scholarpedia.org/

Peer-reviewed, open-access encyclopedia with articles submitted and reviewed by subject experts in scientific fields.

Social Science

Branches of the U.S. Government

You can go directly to a particular branch of government by tapping into the following sites:

White House   http://www.whitehouse.gov

Senate   http://www.senate.gov

House of Representatives   http://www.house.gov

U.S. Department of State:
Background Notes   http://www.state.gov/r/pa/ei/bgn/

Includes information about countries around the world: their geography, government, people, history, political conditions, and more.

FirstGov   http://www.firstgov.gov

This site provides one-step access to online U.S. Federal Government resources. It offers information under various categories, including consumer, defense, education, environment, health, public safety, science and technology, and voting and elections.

University of Michigan Documents Center   http://www.lib.umich.edu/govdocs

This site is a well-organized site for information about the U.S. government.

© 2009. Teacher's Discovery®

THOMAS   http://thomas.loc.gov

THOMAS is a major source of legislative information, including current bills, the Congressional Record, and committee action. In addition, it provides reports, directories, links to other branches of government, and historical documents.

U.S. Census Bureau   http://www.census.gov

Provides population estimates, information about people, business, and geography, including an excellent collection of maps. Find a detailed portrait of the U.S. economy and, for any state, data and statistics about housing, educational level, employment, poverty, and the like. Access American FactFinder for additional facts and figures.

Evaluating Websites

Teachers will often require students to complete evaluation forms for the websites used in their research papers. The evaluation form on page 150 is a modification of one that Marjorie Geldon and Linda Crump created for the Montgomery County (MD) Public Schools. The authors graciously gave their permission to reproduce it here.

© 2009. Teacher's Discovery®

Appendix C

Model Research Papers

The research papers that follow are examples of fine student work. These essays combine creative thinking, careful research, mature writing, and strenuous revision. They exemplify the skills emphasized throughout this manual: narrowing the topic, formulating a forceful thesis statement, finding adequate support from a variety of sources, integrating borrowed material with the author's own ideas, and documenting accurately. In each essay we have double-underlined the thesis statement and have highlighted the method of development (MOD) and major topic sentences to make it easier for readers to see how these important elements are connected.

The first two essays, on topics in the humanities and in MLA style, are by students from Walt Whitman High School in Bethesda, Maryland. The third essay, by a student at the Maret School in Washington, DC, is on a scientific topic and exemplifies APA style. The final paper, composed by two students from Roslyn High School in New York, is an example of an empirical study, or original scientific research, and follows both APA style rules and the IMRAD model.

We are especially grateful to these students' teachers, who not only taught them well but also facilitated the inclusion of their work in this manual. These essays are printed here by permission of the students.

© 2009. Teacher's Discovery®

Portia Cornell

Written by an 11th grade student for an AP English class, this paper analyzes the social role of fairy tales and folktales by examining "Rapunzel" as a child's introduction to the impending changes of adolescence. Of particular interest is this student's excellent use of lead-ins to borrowed material.

Formatting: Citations follow MLA style.

The thesis statement is double-underlined, and the MOD and topic sentences are highlighted to call attention to the organizational structure of the paper.

Cornell 1

Portia Cornell

Dr. Kleppner

AP Eng. Lang., Per 6

15 December 2006

Surviving Adolescence with Magic

The familiar words "Once upon a time" evoke, for many, feelings of nostalgia and warmth; they strike a chord of remembrance. A traditional fairy tale is more memorable than many contemporary children's stories because of its capacity to delve into some of the darker facets of human nature; despite the best efforts of the Victorians to soften and dilute these tales for the nursery, they have kept their folklore essence. This honesty makes the fairy tale appealing to children curious about the realities of the adult world. "Rapunzel," a fairy tale retold by the Grimm brothers, despite its layers of fantasy, is not afraid to "tell it like it is." It deals with some of the important aspects of adolescent growth and development: physical self and sexuality, rebellion, and parent-child relationships. By symbolizing the perils of adolescence, Rapunzel's story of imprisonment and escape provides a child, particularly a young girl, with comfort and guidance as she prepares to enter this stormy time of life.

"Rapunzel" offers a young girl confidence about her changing body and emerging sexuality. Rapunzel's body has tremendous magical power: her tears cure the prince's blindness, and her long tresses allow him to climb up the tower. This power of Rapunzel's body to bring her success reassures the child that her own body will contain such strength (Bettelheim 149). As puberty begins to affect a young girl, the changes it

Cornell 3

(115). Thus the story, while encouraging the formation of new relationships, does not promote promiscuity.

Rapunzel's story also prepares a child for the painful rebellion and process of development that she must undergo to form her individual personality. Pipher describes the difficulties of adolescence as a time when girls "crash and burn in a social and developmental Bermuda Triangle" (19). She adds that without this sometimes painful period of rebellion, a young person, though healthier in the short term, may not develop into a creative, independent adult (92). This stage will be difficult for the child and will be marked by immaturity, struggle, and fear as she tries to make decisions on her own for the first time. But ultimately the struggle shapes her into a more vibrant, thoughtful personality. By following this pattern of struggle and by encouraging autonomy, "Rapunzel" guides young women through this process. Another distinguished folklorist, Maria Tatar, considers Rapunzel's tower the symbolic representation of a mother's protective rules and admonitions. Far from being cautionary elements, as people often interpret them, these warnings become encouragement as they rouse the curiosity and sense of adventure in the young protagonist (166). Rapunzel's imprisonment becomes a metaphor for the strictures a young teenager feels compelled to test, such as her parents' demands for curfews or observance of religious rules, and thus encourages the adolescent to stretch beyond these bonds to become independent.

The tale does not pretend, however, that the transition will be smooth. According to Max Luthi, Rapunzel's story represents a growing process in which the adolescent must first overcome the hardships of loss and danger to achieve lasting happiness

---

Cornell 2

inflicts cause her to feel awkward and unsure. "Rapunzel" helps to curb these insecurities by telling her that, despite these changes, her body still has the means by which she can grow and succeed. Young girls must deal not only with the changes in their outward appearance but also with the emotional effects of adolescence, namely, an emerging sexuality. Psychologist Mary Pipher explains that to come to terms with this newfound sexual self, a girl must learn how to make sexual decisions and to be comfortable with her sexuality, a task that may be one of the major hurdles of young adulthood (205). Rapunzel's golden hair is a complex symbol. Marina Warner points out that "maidenhair can symbolize maidenhead, and its loss, too, and the flux of sexual energy that this releases ... " (374). This sexuality, in the form of Rapunzel's long tresses, enables her to form a relationship with the prince; it lets him reach her in the tower. According to the Grimm version, Rapunzel was "dreadfully frightened when she saw the prince, for she had never seen a man before" (Warner 340). Similarly, an adolescent girl seems to wake up one morning and suddenly "see" the opposite sex as she discovers the different relationships she might have. The fairy tale reminds the young adolescent that she is not alone in her surprise. The young teenager learns that, just as Rapunzel's new sexuality lets her form a loving bond with the prince, these new feelings will let the teenager form similar bonds. "Rapunzel" does not, however, make its message too blatant. Bettelheim argues that since the tale does not mention marriage, nor does it explicitly describe a sexual relationship between the two lovers, one should understand the bond as symbolic of pure love rather than as raw sexuality

© 2009. Teacher's Discovery®

Cornell 5

close to them, and Rapunzel, after her incarceration in the tower, begins to forget her true mother. As Luthi points out, because Rapunzel forgets her parents does not mean she no longer loves them, just that she needs to become emotionally independent of them (114).

In a shift of emphasis, the tale turns from the teenager's perception of a negligent parent to her view of an overprotective, controlling one. Rapunzel moves from her true parents' home into the tower of the witch, where her imprisonment symbolizes the oppression an adolescent often feels from her parents. With this shift, the tale focuses on the main conflict of adolescence. As Pipher maintains, the teenager must give up the protection of her parents' loving relationship just when she feels most vulnerable because of the changes in her life (23). The witch's selfish and seemingly cruel imprisonment becomes comforting to the child who is not yet ready to give up this protection (Bettelheim 148). So "Rapunzel" deals with a teenager's tumultuous feelings about her parents with an exaggerated characterization of all parents' natural desire to keep their child safe from the world.

This approach keeps the balance between encouraging independence and inciting fear and uneasiness. In *The Tower and the Well*, a study of Madame D'Aulnoy's fairy tales, Amy DeGraff observes that a tower often represents a place where the inner self develops. The youth's experience and maturation within the tower suggest that "resistance to parents' authority is a prerequisite to autonomy" (71). This seems equally true in "Rapunzel." Rapunzel must struggle within the confines of the witch's tower until her experience with the prince helps her to break free. The adolescent understands

---

Cornell 4

(112). Citing a Mediterranean version in which the witch kidnaps Rapunzel after biting off her ear, Luthi sees the tale as one of a scary passage into adolescence. For the modern teenager, this kidnapping might be analogous to a change of schools or a parental trip to Europe that leaves the children seemingly abandoned at home. The young must also face the effects of their immaturity. For example, when the witch discovers the two young lovers, the prince rashly flings himself from the tower window, gouging his eyes out on the thorns below. Bettelheim notes the childishness of the lovers' behavior toward the witch, and their despair and hopelessness after she banishes them. These failures, however, are part of the learning process and the development of a responsible self (Bettelheim 149-50). As adolescents ride an emotional roller coaster, they not surprisingly have a tendency toward melodrama. By exaggerating this quality in the prince and Rapunzel, the tale offers comfort and guidance. It cautions a child to think through her problems and to consider consequences rationally. Because the prince eventually regains his sight, the implication is that one can overcome youthful errors and achieve happiness.

For an adolescent, establishing a separate identity means breaking parental ties, and "Rapunzel" sympathizes with the difficulties of the parent-child relationship. It embodies the resentment adolescents often feel toward their parents. Rapunzel's parents are an archetypal "dysfunctional family" as her mother's silly, impractical desire leads to the family's breakdown (Tatar 58). This aspect appeals to a teenager's tendency to suspect that her parents are somehow responsible for her unhappiness. The realization that her parents are not perfect leads the young teenager to feel less

Cornell 7

Works Cited

Bettelheim, Bruno. *The Uses of Enchantment: The Meaning and Importance of Fairy Tales.* New York: Knopf, 1976. Print.

DeGraff, Amy Vanderlyn. *The Tower and the Well: A Psychological Interpretation of the Fairy Tales of Madame D'Aulnoy.* Birmingham: Summa, 1984. Print.

Luthi, Max. *Once Upon a Time: On the Nature of Fairy Tales.* Bloomington: U of Indiana P, 1970. Print.

Pipher, Mary. *Reviving Ophelia: Saving the Selves of Adolescent Girls.* New York: Ballantine, 1994. Print.

"Rapunzel." *The Grimms' Fairy Tales.* Ed. Jacob Grimm and Wilhelm Grimm. Stamford, CT: Longmeadow, 1987. Print.

Tatar, Maria. *The Hard Facts of the Grimms' Fairy Tales.* Princeton: Princeton UP, 1987. Print.

Warner, Marina. *From the Beast to the Blond: On Fairy Tales and Their Tellers.* New York: Farrar, 1994. Print.

Cornell 6

from the tale's message that only as she "breaks free" from her parents' "bonds," can she become an autonomous individual. One final aspect of this story makes it an apt metaphor for parent-child relationships: the fate of the witch. Unlike the stepmother in "Snow White," who must dance herself to death in her red hot shoes, or the stepmother in "Cinderella," who must live out her life as a servant, the witch-like foster mother suffers no act of vengeance. As Rapunzel and the prince have grown out of their adolescent turmoil, they feel no need to punish. So teenagers can hope to grow into independent adults without harboring resentment toward their sometimes-inadequate parents.

"Rapunzel" captures a child's interest with its magic and fantasy and then keeps that interest by avoiding moralistic lectures and by playing up to a naturally adventurous, rebellious youth. Because it deals with serious issues of sexuality and rebellion, the tale is intriguing and memorable not only to a child, but also to young people who are undergoing the transition from adolescence to adulthood. Though a child may not recognize the tale's symbolism or relevance immediately, the deeper meaning of "Rapunzel" may have a profound effect that lasts well beyond the nursery into later years.

© 2009. Teacher's Discovery®

Veronica Foreman

Assigned to write a research paper about the historical or contemporary influences on the composition of Macbeth, this 11th grade Honors English student argues that, through a combination of liberal borrowing from other sources and his own artistry, Shakespeare composed a unique work. The student's synthesis of original source material and literary criticism provides an effective illustration of Shakespeare's debt to other works as well as his own enhancements to plot and character development.

Formatting: Citations follow MLA style.

The thesis statement is double-underlined, and the MOD and topic sentences are highlighted.

Veronica Foreman

Ms. Buckingham

Period 4 Honors English 11B

19 March 2009

Shakespeare's Sources for *Macbeth*

Macbeth, renowned as one of William Shakespeare's greatest tragedies, contains a detailed compilation of thoughts, ideas, and traditions from the Jacobean era. Interested in gaining favor with the newly crowned King James I, Shakespeare depended on sources for *Macbeth* that reflect a clear partiality to the king's Scottish lineage and traditional Scottish views. Shakespeare drew his concepts for *Macbeth* from an array of respected Scottish works, which, despite the authors' frequent fictional embellishments, served as historical accounts of the lives of prominent Scottish individuals. These sources included Holinshed's *The Chronicles of England, Scotland, and Ireland,* Buchanan's *The Chronicles of Scotland, 1582,* and the king's own *Daemonologie.* Although the plot, characters, and concepts he gathered from these documents were vital elements of *Macbeth* and have been noted for their unusually close resemblances, the similarities do not jeopardize the integrity of Shakespeare's text, as he enriched these fundamentals with his own artistry.

Shakespeare's primary source of plot and character for *Macbeth* was the work *The Chronicles of England, Scotland, and Ireland,* by English historian Raphael Holinshed. Shakespeare uses this account, which describes important figures in Scottish history, to provide the majority of his characters' names and titles, a choice that suggests Shakespeare's interest in pleasing King James I. Holinshed's text includes characters named Malcolme, Donwald, Duncan, Makduff, Makbeth, and Banquho, all of whom appear in *Macbeth,* despite the changes

Foreman 1

to some spellings (Satin 536-559). Furthermore, titles present within Shakespeare's work reflect those found within Holinshed's text, including the following: Thane of Glamis, Thane of Cawdor, Thane of Fife, and Prince of Cumberland (Satin 547, 553, 536). Finally, Forres Castle, which is the most prominent location in Holinshed's work, is also the name of the castle in *Macbeth* and provides the setting where Macbeth first meets the witches (538). Holinshed also mentions Birnam Wood and Dunsinane Castle (557), which are the sites in the Shakespearean witches' prophecy of Macbeth's downfall (Shakespeare 5.1.92-94). The names, titles, and locations that Shakespeare references in his work display his indebtedness to Holinshed's chronicle of Scottish history.

Shakespeare uses Holinshed for more than this, though. Major plot parallels are also evident, although the texts themselves are not so similar as to be indistinguishable. Holinshed begins his chapter "Duncan" by describing two battles being fought on behalf of his character King Duncan (Satin 542-43). Shakespeare combines these two battles to provide the conflict that serves as the pretext for his play (Shakespeare 1.2). Holinshed then introduces his character Makbeth, a worthy gentleman who serves courageously in the name of the king. Subsequently, as in Shakespeare's play, returning home from battle Makbeth and his companion Banquho are met by three strange women. Holinshed describes the scene thusly: "The first of them said 'All haile Makbeth, thane of Glammis'. … The second of them said: Haile Makbeth thane of Cawder.' But the third said, 'All haile Makbeth that heereafter shalt be king of Scotland'" (Holinshed "Duncan"). Shakespeare's account of the situation (1.3) is disturbing because it is an exact replication of Holinshed's work. Shakespeare's text then draws from Holinshed's prior section, "Duffe." In "Duffe," Holinshed describes a noble, Donwald, who nurses "an inward malice toward the king … [that] ceased not till, through the setting on of his wife … hee found meanes

Foreman 2

to murder the king." Donwald's wife seems to be the inspiration for Lady Macbeth, as Donwald, whom Holinshed notes having the special trust of the king, seems to be the inspiration for Macbeth. Shakespeare, however, holds Macbeth more personally accountable for his king's murder than Holinshed does Donwald. While Macbeth kills the king himself, and therefore is responsible for both the preparation and the deed, Donwald employs four servants to complete the task and then has them remove the king's body from the castle (Satin 540). Shakespeare does incorporate this idea and revisits the concept of hired assassins in act 3, scene 3 when Banquo is murdered, and again in act 4, scene 2, when a group of murderers execute Macduff's family. Holinshed's accounts, therefore, are a strong inspiration for Shakespeare's text, although Shakespeare conflates scenes, adds details, and changes the chronology and the roles of the principal characters.

Shakespeare also relied heavily on George Buchanan's *The History of Scotland, 1582*, for other major plot events as well as character development within his own play. Primarily, *The History of Scotland, 1582* provides Shakespeare's basis for characters other than Macbeth. For example, Buchanan's chronicle is the source of the departure of Malcolm and his brother after the murder of their father, King Duncan:

The children of Duncan, amazed at this sudden misfortune, their father slain, and the author of the murder upon his throne, surrounded on every side by snares of the tyrant, who sought, by their death, to confirm the kingdom to himself, for some time endeavoured to save themselves by flight, and shifting frequently the places of their concealment. But when they saw they could be nowhere safe, if within reach of his power, and having no hope of mercy from a man of so barbarous a disposition, they fled

Foreman 3

© 2009. Teacher's Discovery®

in different directions, Malcolm into Cumberland, and Donald to his relations in the

Aebudae. (Satin 565)

The similarity is replicated almost exactly in Shakespeare's work, so much so that it nearly challenges the integrity of Shakespeare's work. This potentially indicates that Shakespeare's tragedy is not so much his own fictitious world but rather a historical play drawn from Holinshed's and Buchanan's records. Buchanan's account also provides Shakespeare with the material for the murder of Macduff's family, which Buchanan describes as "Macbeth, having heard of [Macduff's] intended flight, proceeded immediately with a strong force to Fife ... but not finding the Thane, he wreaked his vengeance upon his wife, and his children" (567). The parallel between these sets of characters and events illustrate that Shakespeare, already shown to be heavily indebted to Holinshed, was perhaps overly reliant on exterior sources. Buchanan concludes, explaining that "Macduff having followed the tyrant, [overtakes] him, and [slays] him," thus ending the reign of Macbeth and passing the crown on to Prince Malcolm (Satin 569), and Shakespeare does the same in the final scene of the play. Buchanan's text provides Shakespeare not only with major plot events, but also with the motivations for the characters that surround Macbeth.

Whereas Shakespeare draws the majority of his character and plot elements from Holinshed and Buchanan, his witches can be attributed directly to *Daemonologie*, a text published in the form of a dialogue by King James I. *Daemonologie* served to promote and further establish the king's strong belief in witchcraft and the wicked occurrences for which witches could be held responsible. The witches' discussion of raising storms and causing tribulation for the mortal world in act 1, scene 3 of *Macbeth* is taken directly from King James's belief that witches "can raise storms and tempests in the air, either upon sea or land ... which

Foreman 4

likewise is very easy to be discerned from any other natural tempests ... in respect of the sudden and violent raising thereof" (Rex 47). In fact, Shakespeare incorporates King James's perception of wicked weather through each entrance of the witches with "thunder and lightning" (Thompson 2). Likewise, just as James I asserts in the fifth chapter of *Daemonologie* that the witches have the power to make a man fall ill (Satin 571), Shakespeare's witches boast of their intent to torment a sailor until he is "drain[ed] as dry as hay" (1.3.19) and promise that he will "dwindle, peak, and pine" (1.3.24). In addition to echoing the beliefs of King James, Shakespeare gives voice to a common understanding of his time period, by opening the play with the witches professing that they have been "killing swine" (1.2.2), which is "exactly the kind of thing that accusations of witchcraft in England turned upon" (Thompson 2). Shakespeare's witches are heavily influenced by the convictions of King James and further enhanced by the common perception of witches during this era.

Despite relying heavily on the information he gathered from the aforementioned texts, Shakespeare did in fact change many elements of his play, yielding an entirely new piece of literature. First of all, the witches' repeated presence within *Macbeth* and the malevolent influence that they exert on King Macbeth is "not as flattering to James's political sensibilities as it might be" (Thompson 1). Even though *Macbeth* was written to appeal to King James, the witches' role in the play and his use of them to stir the audience verges on a melodrama that could be seen as exaggerating the king's views. Furthermore, the psychology of Macbeth's wife is distinctive. Despite the presence of mental illness in Holinshed's text, it is only the murderer himself whose guilt drives him to madness. Shakespeare's Lady Macbeth colludes with her husband, helping him plan the murder of Duncan and then ensuring their success by framing the guards when Macbeth cannot, which incriminates her much more than Holinshed does

Foreman 5

© 2009. Teacher's Discovery®

Foreman 7

unique elements and style of Shakespeare's play imparts a well researched, but utterly original text.

The Scottish views and traditions presented in *Macbeth* reflect Shakespeare's interest in the rise of King James I, and Shakespeare's sources for his play were a powerful influence on his work. Despite his reliance on his research, *Macbeth* was innovative and Shakespeare uses it to provide a fresh look at the influence of King James's Scottish background on his time period. Empowered by this influence and these ideas, Shakespeare uses his sources not as a plagiarist, but as a writer who has crafted an original text that reflects not only his debt to prior historians, but also his own artistry and insight into the human condition as well.

Foreman 6

Donwald's wife. Her slow estrangement from her husband and her descent into madness resulting from her guilt consequently makes her one of Shakespeare's most psychologically developed female characters. Shakespeare further distinguishes his Lady from Holinshed's by altering their motivations; whereas Donwald's wife is driven by her own ambition ("Duncan"), Lady Macbeth claims that she is driven only by the hope of helping her husband achieve his goals, because she fears her husband's conscience will ultimately prevent him from attaining the throne (1.5.16-18). The callous strength of Lady Macbeth is unique to Shakespeare's work and defines her as a vehicle to Macbeth's downfall and to her own insanity. These instances show that Shakespeare diverged from his sources in order to provide a richer, more intense story that reflects his own creativity in crafting his play.

Regardless of the importance of Shakespeare's alterations to character and motifs, the most essential aspect setting Shakespeare's *Macbeth* apart from all of the aforementioned works is the style in which it is presented. Shakespeare's use of iambic pentameter, sonnet, soliloquy, metaphor, and verse characterizes his work as something truly independent. These artistic additions distinguish this play as a unique work of art, separate from the historical retellings of Holinshed and Buchanan. Shakespeare creates complex, layered characters with deeply human flaws and weaknesses. For example, as Macbeth contemplates his impending murder of King Duncan over several scenes, Shakespeare uses literary techniques to depict the psychology of a pained man as he sinks toward his own destruction. Macbeth's guilt prior to his action inspires haunting hallucinations and heartfelt regret (2.1.44-77), something that neither Holinshed nor Buchanan impart in their histories. Shakespeare's art, not his research, provides this compelling scene. Although Shakespeare remains faithful to his research, his craft in language and uniquely powerful sense of character develop *Macbeth* into a work of art, not a replication of history. The

© 2009. Teacher's Discovery®

Works Cited

Holinshed, Raphael. "Duffe." *The History of Scotland, An Electronic Edition.* Ed. Gregory
　　Crane. *Perseus Digital Collection.* N.pag. Tufts University, n.d. Web. 5 June 2009.

---. "Duncan." *The History of Scotland, An Electronic Edition.* Ed. Gregory Crane. *Perseus
　　Digital Collection.* N.pag. Tufts University, n.d. Web. 5 June 2009.

Rex, James. *Daemonologie.* 1597. Ed. Yvonne Frost. New Bern: Godolphin, 1996. Print.

Satin, Joseph. "Macbeth." *Shakespeare and His Sources.* Boston, MA: Houghton, 1966. 533-
　　72. Print.

Shakespeare, William. *The Tragedy of Macbeth.* New York, NY: Washington Square, 1992.
　　Print.

Thompson, Edward H. "Macbeth, King James and the Witches." Dept. of English, U of Dundee,
　　Scotland, n.d. Web. 8 June 2009.

Foreman 8

© 2009. Teacher's Discovery®

1

Running head: THE OSPREY

The Osprey: An Overview and Sanibel Snapshot

Jeffrey Dickinson

December 2007

Maret School

Subtropical Zone Ecology

Jeffrey Dickinson

Mr. Dickinson examines the revival of the osprey population in Florida. He supports his argument about the birds' decline and resurgence (under the "right" circumstances) by focusing extensively on the osprey's characteristics and habits.

Format: Written following APA citation guidelines for an ecology class.

The thesis statement is double-underlined, and the MOD and topic sentences are highlighted.

© 2009. Teacher's Discovery®

THE OSPREY

3

osprey pairs. From the vantage offered by these pedestals, the birds can see the ocean waters that they continually fish; the nesting poles are typically constructed where their tenants enjoy a view unobstructed by cliffs, tree branches, TV antenna bars, or other obstacles. Over time, nesting ospreys have come to recognize that these artificial platforms are actually safer than more natural nest sites, usually in fixed branches of dead trees, because the platforms are protected against egg-hunting raccoons by large sheet metal pieces that prevent animals from ascending (M. Westall (personal communication, July 11, 2003). In terms of natural enemies, no creature targets the osprey specifically: its population is kept in check primarily by raccoons and other animals eating the eggs.

Although small mammals and other birds will occasionally enter its diet, the osprey feeds almost exclusively on fish. The hawk's method of fishing is unique. While searching for food, it soars 30 to 100 feet above shallow water. When it spots a fish, the osprey dives swiftly, head- and feet-first, into the water, snaring and gripping its prey with its razor-sharp talons and specially designed foot-pads. Then the osprey beats its wings mightily to raise its fresh catch up out of the water. Once the snared fish clears the surface, the osprey shakes itself off like a wet canine and turns the fish in its talons so that the head and tail of the bird and fish are parallel— and streamlined for flight. As Elphick (2001) points out, the hawk then returns to a favorite roost to eat, pinning the fish down with its talons and tearing at its flesh with its well-shaped beak (p. 217), or it returns to the nest to present the captured meal to its partner and chick(s). Ospreys are usually monogamous: they will remain with the same mate for long periods of time, often their entire life (Elphick, 2001, p. 218). The couple establishes itself through a mating dance in which the pair will circle each other and soar, swoop, and dive together. Once its mating dance is complete, the pair constructs its nest together, a rare practice for birds. The fish hawks construct their substantial nest, which weighs up to 400 pounds, of small tree limbs

---

THE OSPREY

2

The Osprey: An Overview and Sanibel Snapshot

Before the 1960s, the concept of the natural world as an evolved and interdependent web of organisms was ill-formed or nonexistent. Perhaps still reflecting the mentality of the North American frontier, people often thought an animal was worthless unless they could eat it or use its hide or feathers. They hardly ever considered the greater consequences to the organism web as a whole of eliminating a "useless" species. The story of the osprey in recent decades in North America demonstrates our ability to correct poor decisions, as a review of the bird's physical characteristics, habitat, mating and feeding behavior, and threatened survival makes clear. Once universally endangered, the osprey is returning to its former numbers in many places, perhaps led by Florida's Sanibel Island.

The osprey is a large bird of prey, distinguished by its contrasting colors. Its body is dark brown on top and bright white below, dominated by dark brown wings and white legs with sharp black talons. Its white head features a dark brown, horizontal stripe from the eye to the back. Also known as the fish hawk, the osprey is the only raptor whose talons can extend backward, a feature that facilitates its capturing fish. On average, the osprey has a body size of between 22 and 25.2 inches with a wingspan that can reach up to five and a half feet. The design of its bill, typically one to two inches in length, enables it to tear into the flesh of fish when it eats. Closely related to the bald eagle, the osprey presents the same aura of power in its body; the two raptors are often confused, although the osprey's white underside differentiates it.

In North America, the osprey primarily inhabits coastal areas from the Aleutian Islands of Alaska to the Florida Keys. The fish hawk will rarely venture inland, since it searches for food predominantly in water depths of three to six feet. In locating its nest, the osprey prefers a site with a full 360-degree panorama that includes its prospective hunting waters. This preference makes the manmade nesting poles of a place like Sanibel Island, Florida, prime real estate for

THE OSPREY

tissues of fish. Then, as birds of prey ate the fish, they suffered further effects: although the DDT accumulation did not kill them outright, it altered their calcium balance. When they laid their eggs, the calcium structure of the shell became too thin to support even the weight of the growing embryo within the shell (Ehrlich, Dobkin, & Wheye, 1988). As the thinner shells cracked, fewer and fewer offspring survived. The effect of DDT on the osprey population was indeed severe, especially considering the paucity of eggs laid annually. In 1972, after ornithologists established that this problem was decimating the production of young raptors in the higher food-chain levels, the United States banned the use of DDT. Within a decade, the population of birds of prey like the bald eagle and the osprey had rebounded strongly.

On Sanibel Island, Florida, the osprey as an indicator strongly reflects the nurturing environment established and maintained there. Its mayor, Steve Brown, points out that Sanibel Island is known as a nature-focused community (2003). Residents incorporated independently in 1974, splitting decisively from growth-oriented Lee County in so doing, to battle more effectively the strong pressure from developers and other pro-growth factions on its strict environmental zoning policies. As a result of this split, the anti-growth Sanibel Island—once projected by Lee County to support up to 90,000 residents—comfortably supports fewer than 6,000 full-time residents today.

One of Sanibel's leaders in protecting the fish hawk is Mark "Bird" Westall, who provided the following information during an extensive interview (2003). Starting out as a naturalist at the Sanibel-Captiva Conservation Foundation (SCCF) in the late 1970s, Westall noticed that, when an osprey nest was in the way of planned power lines or other improvements on Sanibel, the local power company would simply knock down the offending nest. Westall took an active interest in the osprey and began to monitor bimonthly a comprehensive sampling of 35 nests on the island. Then, in 1981, he launched The International Osprey Foundation

5

THE OSPREY

and large twigs; the interior of the nest is often lined with moss or seaweed (Elphick, p. 219).

The osprey's annual migration dominates its reproduction cycle. Typically, ospreys found in summer in Florida will migrate in the fall to parts of South America, including Chile and Argentina. The couple will return to the same nest each spring at the beginning of mating season. As egg-laying time approaches, the couple will copulate, the male mounting the female's back. Once the eggs are fertilized, the male will feed the female until the day she lays. Ehrlich (1998) reports that, over the next 32 to 43 days, the male and female take turns incubating. Once the eggs hatch, the male hunts and returns his catch to the nest, where the female will feed it to the young before they can fly, typically a period of 48 to 59 days. Because their young have a relatively high chance of survival, fish hawks normally produce only one or two chicks per nest each year. Other animals, like loggerhead turtles, which have only a 1-in-10,000 chance of surviving to adulthood, produce 100–200 eggs per clutch to increase chances of a successful hatch.

Much of the attention focused on the osprey and its numbers in recent decades results from the one-time use in the United States of the pesticide dichlorodiphenyltrichloroethane ($C_{14}H_9Cl_5$), better known as "DDT." "DDT: An Introduction" (Duke University, 1996) notes that DDT was first used in World War II to protect soldiers from malaria; after the war, farmers realized that the chemical combination also worked as an extremely effective insecticide for their farms, virtually eliminating common pests. No one realized that DDT had a downside for another decade or so, when, in the late 1950s, researchers studying worms were surprised to discover DDT levels in the worms high enough to kill the robins that consumed them. Furthermore, in the higher trophic levels of the food chain, the accumulation of a pesticide like DDT builds. The DDT applied to farmers' fields drained into nearby waterways and worked its way through the food chain; as fish gobbled up infected insects, the chemical collected in the

4

© 2009. Teacher's Discovery®

References

Brown, S. (2003). *Attitudes toward growth, business, and the environment on Sanibel Island.* Unpublished manuscript.

Duke University Chemistry Dept. (1996). DDT: An Introduction. In *Cruising chemistry: An introduction to the chemistry of the world around you.* Retrieved from www.chem.duke.edu/~jds/cruise_chem/pest/pest1.html

Ehrlich, P. R. (Ed.). (1998). *The birder's handbook.* New York: Simon and Schuster.

Ehrlich, P. R., Dobkin, D. S., & Wheye, D. (1988). *DDT and Birds.* Retrieved from Stanford University, Birds of Stanford Website: www.stanfordalumni.org/birdsite/text/essays/DDT_and_Birds.html

Elphick, C. (2001). *The Sibley guide to bird life and behavior.* New York: Alfred A. Knopf.

(TIOF) to galvanize volunteers to help rebuild the island's osprey population. Today a committed team of TIOF volunteers counts nests all over the island and tracks the number of chicks fledged annually. The volunteers also actively track such information as which banded birds have returned each spring and which nests are active year to year. Furthermore, TIOF publishes plans for constructing nesting platforms and has proven instrumental in guaranteeing their optimal placement on the island. Thanks in large part to the efforts of Westall and TIOF, the platforms today are widely recognized as an essential contributor to the island's recovered and healthy fish hawk population. Westall notes that today, the local power company "bends over backward" to help Sanibel Islanders put up the poles supporting nesting sites.

Throughout North America generally and on Sanibel Island specifically, the evolving story of the osprey is remarkable. The raptor's striking appearance, its fishing technique, its lengthy migration, and its punctual, monogamous return to the same massive nest each spring fascinate both residents and visitors. However, the osprey was for decades imperiled from both chemical pollution and extreme loss of habitat, until both the federal government's ban on using DDT and the proliferation of manmade platforms began to turn the tide. Thus, the osprey population has resurged generally, in many places even to pre-WWII levels. And nowhere are conditions more suited to the osprey's return than Sanibel Island. An affluent and environmentally aware populace contributing active and committed volunteers, the influence of effective organizations and individuals offering clear direction, and sound anti-growth and other policies have combined to make Sanibel Island an ideal spot for the osprey to thrive. Extensive research has documented the dazzling resurgence of the osprey on Sanibel, making it a model for interested localities throughout the continent to follow.

Running Head: THE EFFECT OF DIFFERENCES

1

The Effect of Differences in Victims' Wealth and Nationality on Altruism

Kevin Xu and Sarah Cha

Roslyn High School

Xu and Cha

This paper is a particularly good example of original research in the sciences, and it includes both a presentation of previous scholarship as well as an exposition of original research, culminating in the authors' ability to draw conclusions and make assertions.

Formatting: Written following APA citation guidelines and IMRAD organization requirements.

This paper is an empirical study, or a report of original research. Although the authors are presenting a thesis in the form of a hypothesis and a method of development in the form of the parameters of their experiment, these elements do not appear in the same manner as most other research papers, nor do they play the same structural role. As a result, a thesis statement is not double-underlined, and the MOD and topic sentences are not highlighted.

© 2009. Teacher's Discovery®

THE EFFECT OF DIFFERENCES 3

The Effect of Differences in Victims' Wealth and Nationality on Altruism

Participation in charities has served as a crucial component of humankind's ability to help others overcome difficulties in life and has raised tremendous amounts of money for those in need. In 1963, Berkowitz and Daniels proposed the social responsibility norm, which holds that people are driven to help those perceived as needy. However, over the years, Americans have donated several times less in relief funds to disasters occurring in poorer foreign countries than for those occurring in the United States. For example, the 2005 Kashmir Earthquake resulted in 14 times as many casualties as Hurricane Katrina, which occurred two months earlier; however, only 14 million dollars was donated to survivors of the earthquake, 30 times less than was received by Hurricane Katrina victims (CNN, 2005). Such patterns of altruism can be attributed to intergroup bias, which is the tendency to evaluate one's own ingroup members more favorably than their outgroup members (Hewstone, Rubin, & Willis, 2002; Tajfel, 1974). This study sought to determine how affluent Americans' desire to help other affluent Americans compares to their desire to help members of needier groups.

Previous research has supported Berkowitz and Daniels's (1963) social responsibility norm. Research that investigated attitudes towards African American job applicants has found that ingroup members have low expectations of outgroup members, perceiving them to be both dependent and needy (Jussim, Coleman, & Lerch, 1987). In their study, participants reported that they were more willing to hire poor African American job applicants than wealthy job applicants, likely due to the participants' sympathy towards the disadvantaged African Americans. Research has also found many participants to be unprejudiced towards the homeless due to awareness of their suffering (Tompsett, Toro, Guzicki, Manrique, & Zatakia, 2006).

THE EFFECT OF DIFFERENCES 2

Abstract

This experiment pitted the social responsibility norm against intergroup bias in an effort to see which would better explain affluent Americans' desire to help natural disaster victims. One hundred eleven high school students were randomly assigned to read about a fictional natural disaster whose victims differed in wealth, status, and nationality. They then completed a survey that evaluated their altruism, sympathy, and just world bias. In line with the social responsibility norm, the participants were more sympathetic to Indonesian victims than American victims. Interestingly, high levels of sympathy, altruism, and just world bias were expressed in all conditions.

THE EFFECT OF DIFFERENCES 4

Contrary to Berkowitz and Daniels' findings, other research has suggested that people tend to favor those more similar to themselves (Norris, Baker, Murphy & Kaniasky, 2005; Perdue, Dovidio, Gurtman & Tyler, 1990; Tajfel & Turner, 1979). Tajfel and Turner's (1979) social identity theory maintains that people's interactions are influenced by a need for self-confidence. This need for self-confidence causes intergroup bias, the tendency to favor ingroup members. Social psychologists have found that intergroup bias protects high ingroup status, provides positive social identity, and satisfies the need for positive self esteem (Tajfel, 1974; Tajfel & Turner, 1979). In addition, research that studied fondness for the pronouns "us" and "them" found that people hold positive attitudes towards ingroup members and are often more willing to help them because it gives them a feeling of assurance that they are a part of the social group (Perdue et al., 1990).

Just world bias is a type of intergroup bias in which people blame victims for their misfortunes and is likely affected by wealth and nationality (Furnham, 2003). The *just world phenomenon* occurs when people view the world as a fair place; hence, victims are viewed to be responsible for their misfortunes in the resulting just world bias (Furnham, 2003). Research has found that perceiving a group as oppressed led people to dislike that group (Uhlmann, Brescoll, & Paluck, 2006). In this study, an overwhelming majority of participants exhibited just world bias due to their awareness of poor African Americans' socioeconomic plight in the United States. Participants described the African Americans negatively and blamed these hypothetical victims for their misfortunes (Uhlmann et al., 2006). Other studies have found that participants perceived African American faces to be more hostile and were unwilling to help them, even after they were made aware of their low social status (Hugenberg & Bodenhausen, 2004). Contrary to these findings, research on public perceptions of the homeless found that certain needy groups

THE EFFECT OF DIFFERENCES 5

are not blamed for their misfortunes (Tompsett et al., 2006). Despite intergroup bias and the social responsibility norm, participants were aware of the plight of the homeless but did not blame them for their misfortunes, likely because of compassion and sympathy.

Previous research has suggested that the effects of intergroup bias are likely to prevail over the effects of the social responsibility norm. Past studies have suggested that humans often tend to be egotistical and are more willing to look out for themselves than others (Epley, Carusi, & Bazerman, 2005). Therefore, it is unlikely that people would be more willing to help outgroup members than ingroup members. Also, racial and socioeconomic differences likely bring about feelings of superiority in a social hierarchy. In particular, nationality differences between people can likely cause racism because the very mention of ethnic differences can arouse feelings of prejudice (Sidanius, Liu, Shaw, & Pratto, 1994; Smedley & Smedley, 2005).

This experiment tested the following hypotheses:

H1: Compared to participants who read about low-income victims of a natural disaster, participants who read about high-income victims will be willing to donate more money.

H2: Compared to participants who read about foreign victims of a natural disaster, participants who read about American victims will also be willing to donate more money.

Method

Participants

The sample for this study consisted of 111 juniors and seniors in a high school located in a suburb within the New York Metropolitan Area. The experiment employed a 2×2 design, and each participant was randomly assigned to one of four conditions. To be included in the sample, participants had to be born in the United States and have family household incomes above $79,000 per year, which is within the top 20% of highest income in the United States.

© 2009. Teacher's Discovery®

THE EFFECT OF DIFFERENCES

Procedure

Prior to conducting the experiment, the approval of the school's Institutional Review Board was obtained. The researchers explained in a scripted set of directions that a recent disaster had occurred in one of four locations: Menteng, Indonesia, Kupang, Indonesia, Arvin, California, or Raleigh Hills, Oregon. Participants were randomly assigned to read one of the four news articles and were told that the focus of the study was to evaluate charity statistics in response to a recent natural disaster. Participants were allotted as much time as necessary to complete the survey and were assured that their answers would be anonymous. All participants completed the survey within ten minutes after receiving it and then filled out a manipulation check in which they answered content-related questions on the wealth and nationality of the victims. Participants indicated how similar they perceived themselves in comparison to the victims in the manipulation check. Three weeks after data collection, all of the participants were debriefed.

Dependent Measures

The first item on the Charity Statistics Survey was answered as an open-ended question in which participants indicated the amount of money in dollars they were willing to contribute towards the victims of the natural disaster. In addition, the Charity Statistics Survey contained two scales developed by Xu and Cha: the Just World Bias Scale and the Sympathy Scale. The items from the two scales were mixed throughout the survey. These items were answered on a six-point Likert-type scale from 1 to 6 measuring the participants' agreements with particular statements. Participants who marked 1 for an item indicated that they strongly disagreed with the statement. Participants who marked a 6 for an item indicated that they strongly agreed with the statement.

THE EFFECT OF DIFFERENCES

Materials

Four versions of a news article were created for this study. Each article described a fictional mudslide. Four real locations that differed in wealth and nationality were chosen to be the scene of the mudslides. Menteng, Indonesia and Raleigh Hills, Oregon are both among the richest (top 10%) towns in their respective countries. Kupang, Indonesia and Arvin, California are both among the poorest (bottom 10%) towns in their respective countries.

In order to minimize potential confounds, the articles were the same except for indications of the wealth and ethnicity of the mudslide victims. All four versions had the same format: an Associated Press news article heading, 327 words, nine paragraphs, identical quotes from victims, and paragraphs discussing identical challenges facing the communities affected by the mudslide. All four versions reported the same number of casualties resulting from the mudslide. Because the disasters, the same amount of damage, and the same costs and extent of destruction. Because the article was adapted from an actual Associated Press news update, the permission of the Associated Press was obtained (AP, 2007).

Two indicators of wealth were inserted into the news articles. For example, an "agrarian town located in a region struggling economically" in a poor location was changed to "a commuter suburb located in a region known for a large informational technology industry" in a wealthy location. Indicators of nationality differences were also placed into the news articles. For example, "an enclave of mostly Americans" in a location representing American ingroup members was changed to "an enclave of mostly Indonesians" in a location representing Indonesian outgroup members.

THE EFFECT OF DIFFERENCES 8

The first scale used was the Just World Bias Scale, in which three items were modeled after Rubin and Peplau's (1975) Just World Scale, which measures belief in a just world, and two items were modeled after Lipkus's (1991) Global Belief in a Just World Scale. An example of an item from the Just World Bias Scale is, "The victims do not deserve any blame in their present situation." Three items on the Just World Bias Scale were reverse-scored, and the scale had an overall reliability of .78 on this study's sample.

The Sympathy Scale was modeled after Davis's (1980) Interpersonal Reactivity Index. All items were answered on a six-point, Likert-type scale measuring agreement to a particular statement, and two items were reverse-scored. One item read, "The occurrence of the disaster did not genuinely upset me," and participants indicated agreement or disagreement. The scale had an overall reliability of .84 on the sample in this study.

Results

Data Analysis

For each dependent variable measured, an overall score was calculated by averaging the total number of items that pertained to the measurement of the dependent variable in the survey. The cutoff for statistical significance was .05.

Three two-way Analyses of Variance examined the effects of the two independent variables (wealth and nationality) on the amount of money participants were willing to donate, sympathy, and Just World Bias Scale scores.

Impact of nationality and wealth differences on sympathy.

Overall, participants were sympathetic towards the natural disaster victims with a mean sympathy score of 4.07 out of 6.00. An ANOVA revealed a significant main effect of nationality on sympathy towards victims of a natural disaster, $F_{(1, 111)} = 6.22$, $p < .01$, $\eta p^2 = .06$. As

---

THE EFFECT OF DIFFERENCES 9

depicted by Figure 1, American participants were more sympathetic towards Indonesian victims ($M = 4.36$) than American victims ($M = 3.81$), which was contrary to the hypothesis.

Wealth did not significantly affect people's sympathy toward wealthy victims of a natural disaster ($M = 4.12$) as compared to poor victims ($M = 4.04$), $F_{(1, 111)} = 0.01$, $p = .98$, $\eta p^2 = .006$. In addition, there was no significant interaction between nationality and wealth, $F_{(1,111)} = 0.81$, $p = .37$, $\eta p^2 = .008$.

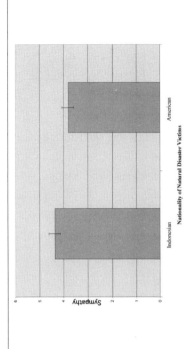

Figure 1. Effect of nationality on sympathy towards natural disaster victims

Impact of nationality and wealth on participants' monetary donations.

The average amount of money each participant reported being willing to donate was $138.45, and 89% of the participants indicated that they would donate to the victims. Contrary to the hypotheses, nationality had no effect on the amount of money participants were willing to donate to victims of a natural disaster, $F_{(1, 111)} = 0.53$, $p = .47$, $\eta p^2 = .005$. Wealth had no effect on the amount of money participants would donate, $F_{(1, 111)} = 0.95$, $p = .33$, $\eta p^2 = .009$. In addition, there was no significant interaction between nationality and wealth, $F_{(1,111)} = 0.05$, $p = .83$, $\eta p^2 = .000$.

© 2009. Teacher's Discovery®

THE EFFECT OF DIFFERENCES

that people are often willing to help those in need. This desire to help the needy likely arouses the participants' sympathy and compassion for the natural disaster victims.

Interestingly, the participants were more sympathetic to Indonesians than Americans. Jussim et al.'s (1987) study on perceptions of outgroup job applicants found that people expect outgroup members to be more dependent and in need of help than their own ingroup members. Therefore, participants likely perceived the Indonesian outgroup members to be needier than the Americans.

While participants were more sympathetic towards Indonesians than Americans, they were equally sympathetic to wealthy and poor victims. Given that wealthy Americans are often perceived to have good fortune with social mobility (DiPrete, 2005), Gilens's (1996) study on common American misperceptions found that people negatively associate poor Americans with laziness. Participants in this study likely may have been more sympathetic towards the Indonesians than Americans because the Indonesians' ethnic identities precluded these stereotypes unique to Americans. Participants may not have perceived the rich Indonesians to be lavishly propitious and poor Indonesians as lazy (Tajfel, 1974).

Impact of Nationality and Wealth on Participants' Monetary Donations

Overall, 89% of the participants were willing to donate money, and the mean figure for donations was $138.45. This high altruism is another indicator of the social responsibility norm and also jibes with the high levels of sympathy expressed. Because the victims were likely perceived as needy, the participants' resulting sympathy likely caused them to be extremely generous.

Even though participants were more sympathetic to the Indonesian victims than the American victims, the amount of money participants were willing to donate was not affected by

---

THE EFFECT OF DIFFERENCES

Table 1

Perceptions of Similarity, Just World Bias, and Amount of Money Participants Were Willing to Donate

Victim characteristics		Perceptions of Similarity			Just World Bias			Amount of Money Participants Were Willing to Donate		
		N	Mean	SD	N	Mean	SD	N	Mean (in $)	SD
Wealth	American	24	2.17	1.20	24	5.33	0.51	24	87.9	108.0
	Indonesian	19	2.89	1.41	19	4.93	1.14	19	132.6	226.0
	Total	43	2.48	1.33	43	5.15	0.86	43	107.7	169.6
Poor	American	29	2.53	1.29	29	5.14	0.91	29	144.1	257.2
	Indonesian	39	2.14	0.95	39	5.14	0.99	39	168.1	286.6
	Total	68	2.32	1.13	68	5.14	0.95	68	157.9	272.7
Grand Total		**111**	**2.38**	**1.21**	**111**	**5.15**	**0.93**	**111**	**138.5**	**238.5**

Impact of nationality and wealth differences on just world bias.

Participants harbored just world bias to all victims of the natural disaster, regardless of nationality and wealth, with a mean score of 5.16 out of 6.00. The amount of just world bias shown towards the victims did not differ significantly between American victims ($M = 5.22$) and Indonesian victims ($M = 5.09$), $F (1, 111) = 1.24, p = .27, \eta p^2 = .009$. The amount of just world bias shown towards the victims did not differ significantly between poor victims ($M = 5.15$) and wealthy victims ($M = 5.16$), $F (1, 111) = 0.01, p = .92, \eta p^2 = .00$. In addition, there was no significant interaction between nationality and wealth, $F (1, 111) = 1.22, p = .27, \eta p^2 = .011$.

Discussion

Impact of Nationality and Wealth on Sympathy

The participants were sympathetic toward all victims, with an average sympathy rating of 4.07 out of 6.00. The results of this study are consistent with Tompsett et al.'s (2006) study and can be explained by the social responsibility norm (Berkowitz & Daniels, 1963), which suggests

© 2009. Teacher's Discovery®

THE EFFECT OF DIFFERENCES
13

As the sample for this experiment was wealthy Americans, it would be valuable to extend this line of research by designing studies that tested whether poorer Americans would be more altruistic towards their ingroup. It would also be interesting to examine whether the social responsibility norm would still exist on poorer Americans' perceptions of wealthy American outgroup members. Lastly, an additional extension of this project would be to investigate whether intergroup bias and the social responsibility norm would be evident if participants were asked to donate to natural disaster victims that differ in race independent of nationality, such as altruism towards African Americans versus Caucasian participants.

Most Americans are undoubtedly aware of the importance of charities in helping others overcome challenges after natural disasters. This research suggests that people are often reluctant to relate to natural disaster victims even if they are sympathetic, altruistic, and clearly similar to them. This reflects the people's attempts to protect their self-confidence by distancing themselves from needy groups, causing sentiments of indifference towards the suffering of others. It is critical in preparing for future disaster relief for people to be aware of their innate tendency to blame victims for their misfortunes as a result of an unbalanced desire for self-confidence. Most importantly, it is crucial to increase awareness that the human tendency to feel indifferent to people who are perceived as different from them has cost billions of dollars in potential relief aid over the years.

THE EFFECT OF DIFFERENCES
12

the nationality or wealth of the victims. This finding is different from past research, which found that participants were more altruistic and helpful toward those similar to them. In past studies, participants were more willing to help perceived ingroup members (e.g., Norris et al., 2005; Uhlmann et al., 2006). One possible explanation for this difference lies in the fact that participants did not perceive themselves to be similar to any of the victims. As participants found themselves to be dissimilar to all of the victims, all victims were seen as outgroup members; it did not matter whether they were Indonesian or American or whether they were rich or poor.

The Impact of Nationality and Wealth on Just World Bias

The participants showed just world bias to all of the victims, with an average score of 5.16 out of 6.00, blaming the victims for their misfortunes. Interestingly, wealth and nationality did not affect Just World Bias Scale scores, suggesting that participants blamed all the victims despite their nationality and wealth status. The participants obviously did not identify with any of the victims, as shown by the manipulation check. The participants likely blamed the victims in an attempt to distance themselves from the victims as a form of self-protection (Hewstone et al, 2002).

Limitations and Further Study

Although a random sample was utilized, all participants were 11th and 12th grade students whose views and ideas might not be representative of the general population of adults. Even though participants were asked whether they would contribute money to the natural disaster victims, participants did not actually contribute money. Therefore, their willingness to donate $138.45 might not reflect the actual amount of money they would donate in reality.

© 2009. Teacher's Discovery®

15

THE EFFECT OF DIFFERENCES

Hugenberg, K., & Bodenhausen, G. V. (2004). The role of prejudice and facial affect in race categorization. *Psychological Science, 15*(5), 342–345. doi: 10.111/j.0956–7976.2004.00680.x

Jussim, L., Coleman, L., & Lerch, L. (1987). The nature of stereotypes: A comparison and integration of three theories. *Journal of Personality and Social Psychology, 52*(3), 536–546. Retrieved from http://www.apa.org/journals/psp/

Lipkus, I. (1991). The construction and preliminary validation of a global belief in a just world scale and the exploratory analysis of the multidimensional belief in a just world scale. *Personality and Individual Differences, 12*(11), 1171–1178. doi: 10.1016\0191–8869(91)9008–L

Norris, F. H., Baker, C. K., Murphy, A. D., & Kaniasky, K. (2005). Social support mobilization and deterioration after Mexico's 1999 flood: Effects of context, gender and time. *American Journal of Community Psychology, 36*(2), 15–28.

Perdue, C. W., Dovidio, J. F., Gurtman, M. B., & Tyler, R. B. (1990). Us and them: Social categorization and the process of intergroup bias. *Journal of Personality and Social Psychology, 59*(3), 475–486. Retrieved from from http://www.apa.org/journals/psp/

Rubin, Z., & Peplau, L. A. (1975). Who believes in a just world? *Journal of Social Issues, 31*(3), 65–86.

Sidanius, J., Liu, J. H., Shaw, J. S., & Pratto, F. (1994). Social dominance orientation, hierarchal attenuators, and hierarchy enhancers: Social dominance theory and the criminal justice system. *Journal of Applied Social Psychology, 24*(4), 338–366. doi: 10.1111/j.1559–1816.1994.tb00586.x

14

THE EFFECT OF DIFFERENCES

References

AP (2007, November 4). Desperation grows as rains pound Haiti. *The Associated Press.* Retrieved from http://www.washingtonpost.com

CNN (2005, September 2). Convoys bring relief to New Orleans as Katrina death toll tops 1000. *CNN.* Retrieved from http://www.cnn.com

Berkowitz, L., & Daniels, L. R. (1963). Responsibility and dependency. *Journal of Abnormal and Social Psychology, 66*(5), 429–436.

Davis, M. H. (1980). A multidimensional approach to individual differences in sympathy. *Catalog of Selected Documents in Psychology, 10*(2), 85–103.

DiPrete, T. A. (2005). Is this a great country? Upward mobility and the chance for riches in contemporary America. *Research in Social Stratification and Mobility, 25*(1), 89–95. doi: 10.1016/j.rssm.2006.05.001

Epley, N., Carusi, E. M., & Bazerman, M. H. (2006). When perspective taking increases taking: Reactive egoism in social interaction. *Journal of Personality and Social Psychology, 91*(5), 872–889. Retrieved from http://www.apa.org/journals/psp/

Furnham, A. (2003). Belief in a just world: Research progress over the past decade. *Personality and Individual Differences, 34*(5), 795–817. doi: 10.1016/S0191–8869(02)00072–7

Gilens, M. (1996). Race and poverty: Public misconceptions and the American news media. *Public Opinion Quarterly, 60*(4), 515–541. Retrieved from http://poq.oxfordjournals.org/archive/

Hewstone, M., Rubin, M., & Willis, H. (2002). Intergroup bias. *Annual Review of Psychology, 53*(1), 575–594. doi:10.1146/annurev.psych.53.100901.135109

THE EFFECT OF DIFFERENCES 16

Smedley, A., & Smedley, B. (2005). Race as a biology is fiction, race as a social problem is real.

    American Psychologist, 60(1), 16–26. Retrieved from http://www.apa.org/journals/amp/

Tajfel, H. (1974). Social Identity and Intergroup Behavior. *Social Science Information, 13*(2),

    65–93.

Tajfel, H., & Turner, J. (1979). The psychological structure of intergroup relations in

    differentiation between social groups. *Annual Review of Psychology, 33*(2), 1–39.

    doi: 10.1146/annurev.ps.33.020182.000245

Tompsett, C. J., Toro, P. A., Guzicki, M., Manrique, M., & Zatakia, J. (2006). Homelessness in

    the United States: Assessing changes in prevalence and public opinion from 1993 to

    2001. *American Journal of Community Psychology, 37*(3), 47–61.

    doi: 10.1007/s10464-005-9007-2

Uhlmann, E. L., Brescoll, V. L., & Paluck, E. L. (2006). Are members of low status groups

    perceived as bad or badly off? Egalitarian negative associations and automatic prejudice.

    Journal of Experimental Social Psychology, 42(3), 491–499.

    doi: 10.1016/j.jesp.2004.10.003

© 2009. Teacher's Discovery®

© 2009. Teacher's Discovery®

© 2009. Teacher's Discovery®